REACHING FOR DREAMS

GARY AND ELIZABETH

REACHING FOR DREAMS

A Ballet
from Rehearsal to Opening Night

BY SUSAN KUKLIN

LOTHROP, LEE & SHEPARD BOOKS
NEW YORK

ACKNOWLEDGMENTS

This book, like the rehearsals it depicts, is a collaborative effort. I would like to thank Alvin Ailey, his dancers, and the crew at the Alvin Ailey American Dance Theater.

After rehearsals, the Ailey dancers would use their lunch break to tape personal stories and thoughts. Sometimes the sessions were one-to-one, but more often than not we would work in threes and fours. We would sprawl out on the floor in "Marilyn's corner." Masazumi Chaya would join us with delicious tastes of Japanese take-out food and Jonathan Riseling would share fruit and give massages. Never were any of them too tired for one more interview, one more *arabesque*.

A special thanks to Susan Hilferty, Timothy Hunter, and Keith Simmons for taking time from their busy schedules to work with me. And just as a ballet cannot exist without backstage participants, a number of behind-the-scenes people helped to make this book possible, including the board of directors: Stanley Plesent, chairperson; as well as William Hammond, Mary Barnett, Ronald M. Bundt, Donald Moss, Calvin Hunt, Adrienne Warren, Penny Frank, and Peter H. Brown. The help given by the staff of the Dance Collection, New York Public Library at Lincoln Center, was invaluable.

When I first learned that Jennifer Muller would be choreographing a ballet for the Ailey company, Peter Woodin, my friend and an ex-Ailey dancer, commented that I would enjoy working with her. Thank you for being right. From the first rehearsals to opening night, Jennifer allowed me to cover her rehearsals without hesitation, without restriction. And long after the rehearsal period was over, she found time from her own activities to give me valuable advice. I could not have done this book without her.

Angeline Wolf was entirely generous with her time, insights, and enthusiasm. Christopher Pilafian could always be counted upon to clarify concepts and bring out one more dimension of the ballet. He conscientiously danced every "Wha-Pa" in the completed text to verify its authenticity. The Works dancers and their executive director, Robert Alpaugh, were caring and supportive during this project too; they answered questions while the Ailey company was on tour.

The help given by Sharon Steinhoff, Barbara Lalicki, Cindy Simon, Carolyn Trager, and Jane Wilson is also greatly appreciated.

Library of Congress Cataloging in Publication Data   Kuklin, Susan.   Reaching for dreams.
1. Alvin Ailey American Dance Theater—Juvenile literature.   2. Ballet dancing—Juvenile literature.   I. Title. GV1788.6.A48K84   1987   792.8'09747'1   86-15356   ISBN 0-688-06316-0

TO BAILEY,
AND TO PEOPLE WHO DANCE.

RENEE AND DANNY

CONTENTS

JENNIFER AND RENEE

SPEEDS

Choreographer: Jennifer Muller
Original score: Burt Alcantara
Costume Designer: Susan Hilferty
Lighting Designer: Timothy Hunter
Project Directors: Angeline Wolf
Christopher Pilafian

THE DANCERS

Marilyn Banks
Debora Chase
Neisha Folkes
Deborah Manning
Renee Robinson
Elizabeth Roxas
Masazumi Chaya
Daniel Clark
Gary DeLoatch
Ralph Glenmore
Jonathan Riseling

ALTERNATE DANCERS

Ruthlyn Solomons
Melinda Welty
Carl Bailey
Max Luna III
Rodney Nugent

CARL

PROLOGUE: THE WARM-UP

Monday, June 24: On a steaming rainy day in June, I rushed down Broadway to the Alvin Ailey American Dance Theater. As soon as I entered through the glass doors, I began to pass classrooms in the Ailey school. The classrooms, which double as rehearsal studios, were filled with students bustling about in various costumes that reflect the many forms of dance taught at the school.

My thoughts raced ahead to the time I would spend here, recording and photographing the process the company dancers and behind-the-scenes people go through when rehearsing a new ballet.

Rehearsals are usually conducted in private. Dancers must feel free to concentrate on their work without outsiders gaping at them, expecting to see a performance. Therefore, it is important that we all become at ease with one another quickly so that my presence and my prying camera do not inhibit or interfere. This is an exciting project for me. Since I was a child, my passion has been the dance.

In Studio 4 in the Ailey school, I find Carl Bailey stretched out in second position, already waiting for the start of the first rehearsal of *Speeds.* It is a thirty-minute piece made up of eight parts or sections. Each section has its own name: "Opening Lines," "Circle Dance," "Trio," "Slow Duet," "Solo," "Fast Duets," "Multiples," and "Coda/Folk Dance."

11

Carl introduces me to a long lanky man and a small stately woman. They are Danny Clark and Renee Robinson, partners in this ballet. They drop their dance bags under the *barre* close to Carl.

As they begin to warm up, Danny tells me, "I've learned to always prepare my body by stretching. Some great things can be done, but a dancer is still human and the body injures easily."

Danny remembers watching "American Bandstand" on television when he was younger. "I would try to dance in front of the set. I also went to see classical ballets. I was fascinated by *The Nutcracker.* When I was in my room, I would turn on music and just move. That helped me express myself. When I was feeling lonely or sad, I would clear the furniture out of the way and dance. I never thought I could do that for a living."

While Carl, Danny, and Renee warm up, Elizabeth Roxas, a delicate young Filipino dancer with long, silky black hair, steps briskly into the studio. She slips out of her high heels and puts on leg warmers.

Elizabeth joins the warm-up. The dancers lie on the floor and do breathing exercises to calm their bodies. Very slowly they stretch out. Then come bigger, broader movements at the *barre*— ballet movements.

Danny says, "I try to make my body alignment perfect— straight, strong, and pulled out. After all that, I loosen up with modern movements." Dancers warm up every working day.

Elizabeth says, "Each year I try to set a new goal. This year it is to project more. To have that sense of maturity onstage. Not just to dance the right steps or the right movement or the right line, but to dance with my whole being."

DANNY

ELIZABETH AND RENEE

Talking and laughing, Jonathan Riseling, Ruthlyn Solomons, Ralph Glenmore, and Debora Chase arrive. They go to a corner at the other end of the studio and drop their dance bags under a piano. Some begin to warm up.

From Ruthlyn's large nylon bag come candy, boxed juices, crackers, and fruit, along with rubber dance pants, leotards, sweaters, dance shoes, socks, and numerous T-shirts.

14

Melinda Welty comes racing in and joins the group. This is Melinda's and Ruthlyn's first week with the senior company after four years with the junior repertory company. They will act as understudies, or alternates, for the other dancers in the ballet. They're nervous. But it is easier for them to begin with a ballet that is new to everyone.

About the Ailey dancers, Melinda says, "Before, I couldn't touch them. I would see them and kinda say, 'Hi.' I'd even dream about them. Now I'm a part of it. Everybody's very warm in the company. I feel welcome."

Marilyn Banks enters, looks about the room with her huge doe eyes, and swiftly walks to the corner, "her corner." She is the senior woman dancer. Her seniority and her reputation as a powerful dancer give her a few privileges. For example, when the company goes on tour, Marilyn has first choice when the dressing and hotel room assignments are given out. She uses this to nourish her strong sense of privacy.

With privilege comes responsibility. Marilyn and other senior members make it a point to support junior dancers, just as they were guided when they began dancing. When Marilyn has something to say, the others listen. Today she looks around silently. Still chewing gum and wearing her Walkman, she begins her warm-up.

Jennifer Muller, the choreographer who created *Speeds* for her own company, The Works, arrives. Already barefoot, wearing a black leotard and leg warmers, Jennifer sets up her own area next to a tape recorder on a long bench in front of the wall-to-wall mirrors. She carries a large thermos of coffee.

Jennifer says, "While working with my own company, I have all the dancers in my head. I can see what they look like and how they move. I call it my little mental movie. And I watch them. I choreograph by thinking of individuals. I take their personalities into account—what they're capable of expressing."

In order to "put *Speeds* on" the Ailey company, Jennifer had to find the right people to fit predefined parts. To help, two dancers from her company, Angeline (Ange) Wolf and Christopher Pilafian, have been acting as assistants. All three have been dancing in *Speeds* since it was created eleven years ago. They know every part.

There are eleven dancers in *Speeds.* Most dancers in the cast learn two parts, their primary role and a second or alternate role. Five extra performers are cast in several parts in case someone is ill or injured.

Before this rehearsal period began, Jennifer had everybody in the Ailey company dance a series of steps. Later, Ange and Christopher sat with Jennifer at her kitchen table and worked for hours on the casting: Who is right for this role? How would so-and-so look in this section?

"It's like a crossword puzzle," says Jennifer. "Does she move fast? Does he move slow? Does she have the stature? Does he have the romance? Does she have the delicacy? Does he have the zip?"

Debby Manning, Neisha Folkes, Max Luna, and Rodney Nugent enter the studio. Waving hello to the other dancers, they gather around Jennifer, who introduces them to me.

Gary DeLoatch saunters in. Happy and relaxed, he shoots Jennifer a big smile. "Morning, Jenny. Morning, y'all." He walks toward the group stretching and talking under the piano. Besides being a senior member of the company, he frequently teaches master classes when the company is on tour.

Offstage Gary is not afraid to speak up for himself or—more likely—on behalf of other dancers. Onstage he is dependable and consistent.

About Gary, Jonathan says, "It's nice to have somebody as confident as he is onstage with me. He gives so much when he dances that it forces others to give as well. He doesn't have to say anything—he keeps us on track just by being there."

16

Another highly respected senior member arrives. He is Masazumi Chaya, called Chaya. His face lights up when a young dancer does a sequence well. He tenderly refers to other members of the company as his children. "I studied dancing because I wanted to be an actor. I didn't want to be a dancer," Chaya says. "It was too hard. I took ballet and joined a company in Japan, staying there two years. My father is a doctor; my mother is a nurse. They were shocked that I was going to be in the theater business. 'Those people!' they said. Because there are few male dancers in Japan, I was getting lots of jobs. I wanted to make sure I was good. Where's the best place to find out? In New York City, of course.

"When I heard that Jennifer Muller was going to put *Speeds* on our company, I was excited. I had had a great time dancing in a previous ballet she choreographed especially for us called *Crosswords*. I'm glad she cast me in this piece.

"Our company is trained in modern dance, but we do not do much of it. Most of the ballets we do are jazz oriented. It is easy to forget how modern dance feels. This will be a good challenge for everybody."

CHAYA

1. FIRST, THE STEPS

Before rehearsal begins, Keith Simmons arrives. He is one of two company stage managers. A stage manager runs the technical part of the ballet, which includes the lights, the music, and the curtain. Therefore Keith must learn the music and light cues as well as everyone's entrances and exits. Among his many duties, Keith takes attendance.

"Morning, ladies and gentlemen. Everybody here?" Keith has a soothing voice. He is always calm—even when things begin to get tense. Dressed in a businesslike shirt and tie, he carries a clipboard with rehearsal schedules and attendance lists.

Speeds will rehearse five days a week, from eleven o'clock to one in the afternoon for the next seven weeks—except next week, when the troupe is on tour. Finally, during three performance days at Wolf Trap in Virginia—August 12 to 14—they will premiere *Speeds* along with two other new ballets: *Lament,* choreographed by Louis Johnson, and *How to Walk an Elephant,* by the post-modern choreographers Bill T. Jones and Arnie Zane.

All the dancers who are in the ballet must be present promptly for all rehearsals. Keith checks his attendance list and leaves the studio for his office upstairs.

Christopher says, "During these rehearsals the Ailey dancers will make *Speeds* their own." He acknowledges that learning Jennifer's distinctive style will be difficult because the two companies approach dance differently.

18

Alvin Ailey bases his choreography on the techniques of Lester Horton, a pioneer in modern dance. Ailey combines ballet, modern, jazz, and even tap in his ballets. His works are theatrical and athletic.

Jennifer is a spiritual descendant of Doris Humphrey, a dancer-choreographer-teacher who experimented with new ways of developing movement in modern dance. Her ballets tend to be lush and psychological.

Jennifer says, "First we teach the steps." The steps used are like words in a story. Combinations of steps are called phrases. A phrase is like a sentence. It has a beginning, a middle, and an end, and it usually makes a simple dance statement. A series of phrases is a sequence: a paragraph. A series of sequences is a section: a chapter. The sections make up the ballet.

Everything must be taught step by step. Jennifer says, "Even though video is playing an increasing role as a teaching aid, dance must be passed down from person to person in order to convey the entire energy of the piece, the correct energy."

The ballet begins with an empty stage. The dancers will enter very slowly in a straight line downstage and snake around, changing speeds until they reach the back of the stage.

When Jennifer contemplated the lineup for "Opening Lines," she wrote many notes. Who would stand next to whom? Her decisions were based on the individual's height, body shape, and energy level.

Once in the studio she tells the dancers where their places are in the line. "Number one is going to be Chaya. Number two is Elizabeth. Three, Marilyn; four, Ralph. Five is Debora. Six is Gary. Seven, Debby. Eight, Jonathan. Nine, Neisha. Ten, Renee. Eleven, Danny." All eleven dancers line up, facing the mirror. The five alternates—Melinda, Ruthlyn, Carl, Max, and Rodney— go through the movements on either side of the line.

Jennifer says, "Okay, let's walk it first." The choreographer leads the dancers through a few steps. Then she explains, "At a fixed time, a specific dancer will say, 'Change.'" That word represents a wash of the stage. Whenever it's said, the dynamics of the dance change dramatically. In fact, the theme of this ballet is change—of velocity, direction, and dynamics.

In dance the standard tempo is counted in eight beats. The dancers do not dance "up to tempo," or full speed, in the beginning rehearsals. The speed picks up gradually.

Jennifer sets the speed by counting. The dancers start dancing at "one," but Jennifer starts counting a new sequence at "five" to give the dancers the few beats they need to feel the tempo before beginning.

The counting also is a time cue for the specific steps. A choreographer may tell a dancer, "The *arabesque* is on 'four' and the step out of it is on 'five.'" Sometimes a tempo is kept, not by counting, but by the rhythm of the body or the breath.

As the choreographer works, she uses balletic words to explain what to do: *plié, relevé, rond de jambe, attitude*. The dancers know these basic steps and are quick to pick up phrasing. What they have to learn is the sequence of phrases and Jennifer's distinctive variations on a position.

Rehearsal, to Renee Robinson, means learning many new things. She is observing already that Jennifer's style has a noticeable roundness to it.

Jennifer says, "The Ailey company is *wonderfully* aware of the fact that my style is different. They're fascinated by what makes it so. They appreciate that the body can soften, that it can be off balance if the hips are centered. They see that my *plié* is much softer. It is a more vulnerable *plié*. It gives into the floor more. Their curiosity helps. They're meeting me halfway."

CHAYA, ELIZABETH, MARILYN, RALPH, DEBBY, GARY, JONATHAN, NEISHA

21

DEBORA, DANNY, CHRISTOPHER (CENTER), AND ELIZABETH

Along with the names of steps, Jennifer peppers her statements
with funny make-believe words that correspond to the rhythm of
the music. "Wha-Pa . . . Hep! Hep! Hep!" The dancers, in effect,
are learning a new language. They pick it up fast. Once in a while
they will miss a step or bump into one another. A simple "sorry"
is called out, and the dancers keep going.

"Change!" "Change!" "Change!" each dancer says in turn, while
walking forward. Most practically whisper the word. Dancers are
trained to talk with their bodies, not their voices; therefore it is
unnatural for them to speak while performing. Jennifer lets it pass.
  "Don't go above this line." Jennifer shows the dancers how far
downstage they may go during this sequence.

22

"Change!" "Change!" "Change!" they each say.

"Follow the leader, everybody," calls Jennifer, and she lets out a long, billowing laugh.

Jennifer's laugh is infectious. It starts low, deep in her diaphragm, and grows bigger and bigger, like the movements at the *barre.* When she laughs, the company laughs with her. Jennifer never laughs at anyone except, perhaps, herself. The Ailey dancers delight in that engaging characteristic. It eases the tension that long, repetitive rehearsals often produce.

The choreographer stands in front of the group, drinking coffee as she talks. Ange and Christopher are on either side of her, demonstrating the steps and leading the dancers in front of the large mirror. The two feel free to point out a well-executed movement or to make a correction. "From now on, keep on a sharp diagonal so that all the forward feet are on the same line," says Ange while dancing along.

"Front, front, back, back, up, sit . . . THEN follow Chaya," sings Jennifer in eight counts. "ONE and, out of the bottom of your eyes, check to see that your feet are on the same line as we turn." The dancers follow.

After the first hour, precisely as the second hand hits twelve, the stage manager reappears at the door. The dancers stop everything and take the five-minute break that their union requires. Some quickly exit for take-out food or coffee. Others go off by themselves to rest. Two or three dancers joke and laugh together.

Neisha Folkes takes the time to review the movements she learned during the previous hour. When the dancers tease her, she says, "I'm dancin' on my five." Neisha remembers seeing her first live dance concert when she was thirteen years old. It was the Alvin Ailey company. From that day on, she says, "I thought, I want to dance."

Once Neisha had that goal, nothing could stop her. She figured out exactly what to do and how to do it. She auditioned and was admitted to the High School of Performing Arts in New York

City. When she graduated at the top of her class and was awarded scholarships to several colleges, she chose the Juilliard School.

After the second rehearsal hour Keith appears at the door to indicate time is up. Jennifer finishes the phrase she has been teaching. "That's it! Thank you," she says.

The dancers gather around her, clapping as a show of appreciation for an enjoyable rehearsal. Then they quickly pack up their belongings and scatter in different directions. The Ailey dancers take an hour lunch break before attending other rehearsals. Jennifer, Ange, and Christopher go to The Works' studio to rehearse with their company.

Thursday, June 27: Christopher begins teaching a step. He says, "We are going to do a jump. After you've landed, we are going to soften the legs here." He points to his thighs and watches in the mirror as the dancers jump. Jennifer walks among the dancers correcting body placement.

The dancers watch their own movements and one another's as well. In this way they help their fellow dancers and improve their own dancing techniques.

The choreographer and her assistants break the company into groups and rehearse various sections. Jennifer rehearses the section called "Slow Duet." It is a slow, sensuous dance about two people who meet, become lovers, and then part. Danny and Renee are the lovers in this section, and Gary and Elizabeth are their alternates.

Danny is tall. When he dances with Renee, he has to bend far down and stretch his legs in order to meet her. Renee says, "I'm comfortable dancing with Danny because we talk things out. But it would be more convenient if he were closer to me in height. Because our heights are drastically different, we have to say, 'Hey, wait a minute,' and we adjust."

The dancers must be comfortable in the shapes that they dance. If they aren't, the piece won't work. A key to the entire process is

CHRISTOPHER AND JENNIFER

comfort. Jennifer will say to them, "This is the weird shape; here comes the weird shape." So far, to the Ailey dancers, her shapes *are* weird. Acknowledging this makes it easier for the dancers to adjust to unfamiliar body positions.

The choreographer directs Danny and Renee, "Soften your body down. It is as if the woman is trying to touch the man on the side of the face but there is always a little bit of space between them." She has Renee place her hand on the front of Danny's thigh. Danny moves back a step, taking Renee with him.

"Danny has those gorgeous long arms and legs. He's going to look spectacular in 'Slow Duet,'" says Jennifer. "It is wonderful to see what those long limbs will do with my ballet."

RENEE AND DANNY

26

First and foremost, Danny tries to do the choreographer's movements as accurately as possible. Next, he tries to make his partner look good. "I want to make her feel comfortable." After a lift Danny will ask, "Was that okay for you? Did I hold you too tightly? Did you have enough support?"

Then he considers the feeling the dance conveys. The way to dance a "feeling" is to call on his own experiences. For example, "Slow Duet" is about a yearning love affair. Danny says, "When I see Renee, I imagine somebody that I once wanted to have a relationship with. During each movement I try to sense that person and recreate those emotions.

"I like the very beginning of 'Slow Duet,' when Renee contracts her body toward me and I start leaning away while my face is toward her. It symbolizes a yearning feeling. I like that. I like duets that are calm, because sometimes I feel so pressured to do a good job that I forget how pleasurable dancing is."

Jennifer continues directing both couples in "Slow Duet." "You may be a little far apart. Soft . . . as if you want to reach him with your body, with your face. Beautiful, beautiful!" The men move their faces close to their partners' lips.

As Elizabeth dances, she concentrates first on Jennifer's directions, and second on Renee's execution of the steps. Elizabeth is small and delicate, and Gary is massive. Generally the man in a duet supports the woman, but in some movements in this ballet the woman supports the man. Elizabeth checks herself in the mirror to make sure she is in the right position to help Gary hold his balance.

Elizabeth says, "I trust Gary entirely. I know that when I jump, he will be there to catch me. That is the respect dancers must have for each other. This is the first time we are partnering together, and so far it has gone very well." When a movement does not work, they do it again and again until it does.

Ange demonstrates a phrase with Danny while Renee watches.

Gary and Elizabeth work behind them. Though Gary and Elizabeth will not be dancing *Speeds* on opening night, they will do so while on tour. The ballet must be learned perfectly. As far as Gary is concerned, when he's learning an alternate part, "It's my role!"

Gary says, "There is a big difference between dancing 'Slow Duet' with Elizabeth and with Renee, because they are different people. First, they are not alike physically. Elizabeth is fleeting. Renee is earthy. I have to be aware how their legs and hips turn open, how to maneuver when holding them. Second, I must figure out how much they're going to let me do and how much they're going to do on their own.

"We don't talk about it. That part comes instinctively, by gently touching and moving to the beat. My partners usually find out that I'm running things. It might be because I'm older, I've had more dance. So they give me that." He laughs. "In any event, I make it clear that before you put your hand on me, I'm running the show."

Jennifer stops the couples. "Let's take our 'five' now, and then we'll put this part to music."

Choreographers work with music in various ways. Some choose music and then adapt a ballet to it. A choreographer may piece together different scores. Others commission a composer to write something new.

When Jennifer creates a ballet, she begins her work in silence. "I think, What music do I hear? And then I try to find the person to write that music."

For *Speeds*, Jennifer asked composer Burt Alcantara to collaborate with her on the electronic score. He attended rehearsals at Jennifer's studio. Afterward they would talk about the ballet. He would play a little music, and they would talk some more. They decided what parts he should support with his music and what parts would do without. The rhythm of each section was chosen. He worked with a synthesizer and two tape recorders. He made all the musical lines and dubbed them over one another until he developed the sound they wanted.

After their five-minute break, the "Slow Duet" dancers work to Burt's music. They immediately react to the haunting, rich sound.

Danny tries to create a special feeling for every single movement. He says, "I don't have it all blocked out yet because I'm just beginning. I watch what happens to my body spontaneously. I want to learn how each movement makes me feel and then I attach an image to it. Today I'm imagining a starry summer night on an empty beach.

"If I find that there's a rough spot, I say to myself, I think this is dead; I don't feel anything here. When that happens to me, I know that the audience won't feel anything either. I go back and think up more images."

Danny's partner, Renee, lets her body respond directly to the luxurious shapes in the choreography without using images. She says, "Because the deepness of the *plié* is so very dramatic, a great deal of feeling comes into play. I love this. I'm already expressing something without even doing anything with my face. And all the twistings . . . it's so female."

When Alvin Ailey is in town, he makes it a point to visit part of each rehearsal. A strong, intense man with warm eyes and a gentle smile, he usually sits alone in front of his dancers. He never interrupts. He watches every move.

Ailey's vision was to start an interracial dance company that would perform great American ballets and commission new ones. In 1958 he started his company with seven dancers at the 92nd Street YMHA in New York. Now there are more than thirty dancers in his company. He also heads a school and a repertory group. Over the years more than 150 ballets by more than forty-five choreographers have been presented. About fifty of the ballets are by Ailey himself. Many companies perform only the works of a single choreographer. Ailey encourages his dancers to work with many choreographers. He tells them, "This is not the last place. We have to grow from here."

Sometimes Bill Hammond, the executive director of the company, watches the rehearsal with Ailey. Bill's job is to make a reality of Alvin Ailey's vision. He works with the board of directors and the staff. He sets the budget, reviews and writes contracts, arranges tour dates, and takes care of the thousands of inevitable details. He says, "I like to leave my office, with the phones ringing and contracts piled on the desk, and drop in to the rehearsals. It is important to me that the dancers know me. I like to feel that if they have a problem, I'm somebody they can talk to."

GARY, RUTHLYN, JONATHAN, JENNIFER, NEISHA, RENEE, DANNY, AND ALVIN AILEY (FOREGROUND)

Friday, June 28: The dancers arrive laughing and chatting about all they have to do today. Some are carrying suitcases in preparation for the week of performing and taping for "Dance in America" in Switzerland. They begin their warm-ups.

Jennifer will continue working with "Slow Duet." Ange and Christopher will work with other groups of dancers on different parts. During the course of the rehearsal, Ange or Christopher partners Jennifer in order to demonstrate a particular movement.

Jennifer tries to explain a difficult phrase. "Here the woman has a hard job. First she sits. Then she rises up and reaches toward the man." Jennifer reaches up to find Danny's rib and says, "You need to find his rib, here. And then," she continues to explain to Renee, "you can rise up beside him. Go straight up. Now tilt . . . there we go. *Yes!* That's it!"

During rehearsal Connie Singer, the assistant to the costume designer, comes to the studio to take measurements. Jennifer says, "When I began *Speeds,* I knew the costumes would be street clothes; I knew that they would be white; and I knew that the dancers would change some part of their clothing every time they danced a new section of the ballet." With that in mind, she chose designer Susan Hilferty to create costumes from ordinary clothing.

People generally do not jump high in the air while turning, or do a split, when wearing new white linen pants. Susan will have to retailor each outfit to allow the dancers to move.

As the rehearsal ends, Keith comes down to the studio and calmly announces that the bus will leave for the airport in two hours.

Two hours! Carl says he hasn't packed yet. Danny has to go to the bank. And Gary must shave. Dancers race out of the studio with a welter of questions: "Where's my passport?" "Where's my checkbook?" "What season is it in Switzerland?"

JONATHAN, MELINDA, AND CONNIE

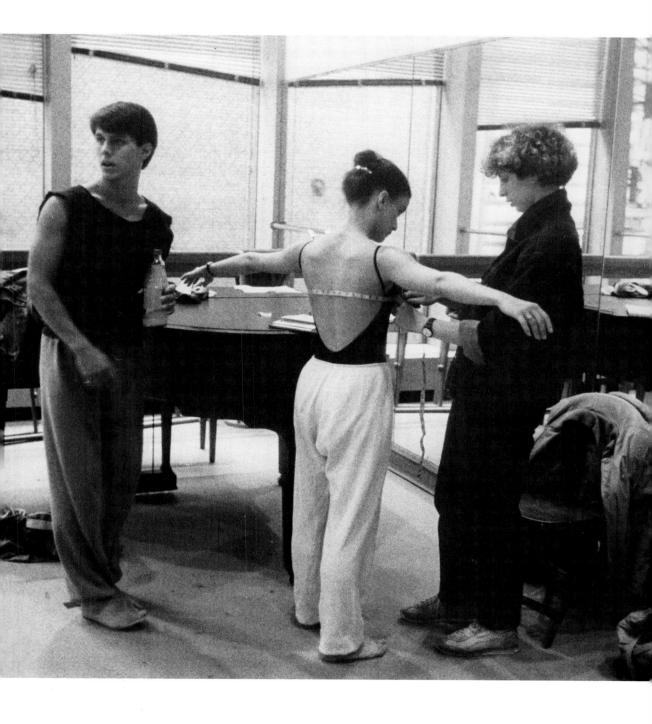

2. AND AGAIN ... THE STEPS

*M*onday, *July 8:* Jennifer says, "When I create a ballet, first comes the vocabulary period to determine the kind of movement or style that is appropriate to the piece. Then comes the laying-out period, and that includes choosing the steps. I ask myself: When will I use a particular step? With whom will I use it? The answers to these questions determine the floor patterns and the groupings. I decide how certain steps will connect and interact with one another. That determines the rhythm. After that I ask, Why will I use this step? The dynamics and tension of the ballet are reflected in the answer.

Third is the period in which I sit back and look at my ballet and start chopping away and forming it. That's where artistic choice comes in. When putting the pieces together, so much of the unconscious comes into play. It is a big struggle to become more objective. Do I try to bring the dance back to what I visualized? Or is it becoming enough of its own creature that I must let it go? The finished piece will never be exactly as I envisioned it, but how different will it be?"

It will take time for the dancers to discover every detail of the ballet. Christopher says, "When they talk with us about the piece, the ballet starts to become their own. We encourage that process."

Gary is becoming impatient. "I wish they would hurry up and run the whole ballet. I know there are still some parts to be taught, but I want to see it all. Maybe it's because I've choreographed myself that I look at the whole idea, not just the individual steps."

Jennifer says, "Choreographers learn through an apprenticeship—by observing and working with other choreographers. That's how we develop our craft."

Throughout the rehearsals Gary and Neisha listen to the way Jennifer explains a movement, study her use of space, and watch how she puts phrases together. "I pick up fast. I can anticipate what Jennifer's getting at," says Gary. "I sometimes wonder what is taking the others so long. That's because the other dancers concentrate on foot movements or hand movements. I don't worry about those. I look at the whole picture."

Wednesday, July 10: During part of the rehearsal, Jennifer works with Chaya and Max. Although Max Luna is young and new to the Ailey company, he has been a professional dancer for fifteen years. His job is to understudy Chaya's role. "I haven't danced every section yet. I'm still working on continuity, sequence, and the steps. It's getting there. There is much to master."

Max is learning six new ballets. He says he's not worried. At times, he has had to learn a ballet in the afternoon and dance it that evening. As long as the choreographer is clear about what is needed, he just goes out and does it. Also, he is delighted to be covering Chaya.

Chaya says, "I arrived in New York with the dream of performing on Broadway. I went to many auditions. I never got a part. First of all, you must have a visa to work, and I didn't have one. Sometimes the Broadway producers would say, 'Oh, Mr. Chaya, we like you very much, we like your work, but we cannot hire you. You are not the right type.' I was running out of money. To eat, I cleaned people's apartments.

MAX, JENNIFER, AND CHAYA

"One day a friend invited me to come to an audition. 'What should I bring?' I asked. 'Nothing, just come.' But I took my jazz pants and jazz shoes, just in case. It turned out to be a ballet audition. The girls had on *pointe* shoes and pink tights, and the boys were all in white ballet shoes and black tights. Oh no! I was embarrassed. But at that time I didn't have a job and had no money, so I thought of it as a free class. I danced. They hired me."

Chaya is a natural teacher. He watches over the less experienced dancers and works with them every chance he gets. After Chaya and Debby dance with Jennifer, Max and Ruthlyn work with her on the same movements. Chaya looks carefully at Max's performance and offers suggestions.

Friday, July 12: Neisha arrives at the studio early to take a beginner's class in Horton technique, which isolates and stretches every muscle.

Once the *Speeds* rehearsal begins, Jennifer works on a section of the ballet with Marilyn, Ralph, Debora, and Debby. Alternates Ruthlyn and Melinda watch and move along with the dancers on one side of the studio. Carl dances behind Ralph.

In this ballet Carl is in the second cast. He understudies both Gary and Ralph. Having two parts is exciting. A most versatile performer, Carl can quickly switch into the personality required by the role. "I watch what the first cast does with the parts and then challenge myself. Even though I'm dancing their roles, I make sure that I remain my own person on the stage.

"Everybody likes to be in the first cast and have the joy of being the first to do it. After the disappointment of not being first is over—it takes about a day for me—it's cool."

Tuesday, July 16: Susan Hilferty, the costume designer, is shopping in New York's garment district. "I am looking for white fabrics that will survive. First I tried fabrics made from acetate, which was terrible for this task. It shreds."

Each dancer has only one hour of fitting time for all the costume changes. Susan is feeling the pressure of having to select and retailor all the costumes in such a short time. She cannot take the dancers to a store to try on possible outfits. Much time is spent buying things, taking them to the studio, trying them on, seeing if they work, and, if not, returning them. Susan and her assistant shop and fit the dancers every day. They race in and out of boutiques and fabric stores with portfolios that list dancers' measurements and descriptions of their roles in the ballet.

Susan majored in painting at Syracuse University. Not trusting her future as a painter, she minored in fashion design. She likes to sew. "I always made my own clothes. I learned how to drape and make patterns. One of the reasons I went to Syracuse was that they have a drama school. I acted in high school. After college I

spent a year in England at St. Martin's School of Art. While I was there, I went to the theater. It was there I first became fully conscious of design as something integral to the production of a play."

The choreographer often starts with a costume idea. In this case it was white street clothes. Some choreographers are quite specific about the costumes and some are not specific at all. The costume designer must figure out how to make that idea come to life. That's Susan's job.

Thursday, July 18: In the studio Christopher explains the feeling of a trio he is teaching to Chaya, Neisha, and Ralph: "The mood is happy, pleasant, formal."

They work for a while until Jennifer joins them. "We're going to press ahead," she says as she places each dancer on the spot where they are to learn a new sequence. "Neisha will be the first one. She will cut away from the others and begin a series of half turns in a diagonal direction. Ralph will step into Neisha's space as soon as she takes off." Once they finish dancing the sequence, Jennifer says, "GOOD! . . . One more time!" As she begins her count, she increases the tempo noticeably.

MAX, CHRISTOPHER, AND NEISHA

When dancers do a sequence incorrectly, they do it again. And when it's correct, they do it again, just for luck.

Ange is watching, helping, encouraging. "Nice curve down here—palm facing in. WHOOOPS!" she says as Neisha takes a tumble. Ange gives "Neish" a hand—and a hug. She does the movement again. Then the alternates try the same movements.

Neisha is at ease with the three teachers. She isn't always that way. "I'm very sensitive. If you don't say the right things to me, I withdraw. I feel that Jennifer knows how to bring dance out of me. She makes me feel like such a wonderful dancer that I know I'm going to shine."

While many dancers are not as sensitive to criticism as Neisha, all are sensitive to the temperature. They need to keep warm in order for their muscles to remain loose and relaxed. Layers and layers of clothes protect them: leotards, T-shirts, leg warmers, rubber exercise suits, socks, and perhaps a scarf or a sweater or two. During rehearsal clothing is constantly flying off to the sides of the studio or being whipped back on.

Keith comes to the studio. It is time for the five-minute break. Jennifer rushes to finish one last phrase. When it is done, Jonathan runs out to a store and returns with fresh fruit for Ruthlyn, who is always hungry.

Once the rehearsal resumes, those who are not working with the choreographer and her assistants go over sections of the ballet alone. Marilyn and Jonathan go to Marilyn's corner to rehearse their duet whenever they can. Sometimes a dancer will take a moment to relax. Dancers must tune in to the needs of their bodies. They understand when it is time to just stop. And they rest in the strangest positions.

Modern choreographers often ask a dancer to represent an abstraction—a line, a position in space. The dancer's personality must vanish so the body shapes can be clearly seen.

Jennifer emphasizes the human condition in her ballets. "I see

the body as an envelope for emotions: joys, fears. . . . Living beings are on that stage. Their bodies are such expressive instruments. They reach people at the visceral level. How can you cut humanity from the dancers? How can you cut out those spirits, those hopes, those desires? My choreography is definitely a mirror of the psyche."

The Ailey dancers can adapt to abstract or humanistic choreography. Alvin Ailey brings together dancers who not only have varied training, such as ballet, modern, and Broadway, but also different nationalities, races, and religions.

Chaya says, "People bring their own personal background to Alvin's style. He likes that, he really likes that. He likes people who have various histories."

Elizabeth

41

Monday, July 22: Jennifer begins work on a complicated section called "Trio." She chose her trio—Debora, Debby, and Gary—without knowing that all three dancers are from Philadelphia. But although the company calls them "the Philly connection," this is the first time they have been featured together.

Debora says, "From the very beginning I felt we three had a definite harmony. I don't dance with Gary that often. Being able to fall into a natural rhythm with him feels good to me. Debby and I went to school together. There are certain things we can bypass because we already connect. That makes it more fun."

The dancers are eager to get a step right the first time. That doesn't always happen. During one particularly difficult sequence, the choreographer sympathizes, saying, "This is frustrating. There's no question about it." Everyone laughs.

Gary sighs extravagantly, hands to his heart. "I feel better now."

GARY, DEBORA, AND DEBBY

42

As Debby dances, her eyes are fixed on the mirror. Eventually she stops her partners and says, "There's something about this leg. It doesn't look good." She can tell that something is not working, but she needs others to figure out exactly what is wrong.

To teach the movement correctly, Jennifer dances the sequence with Christopher. She first recalls how each shape "feels" and then captures that feeling with words. She does the same step with Debby. Finally the dancers do it themselves while Jennifer watches. "That's it!" she says.

The three dancers learn the complicated phrases in four rehearsal periods. They want to run through the entire routine. Jennifer says, "Why not give it a try?"

After the first run-through, Gary and Debora lie on the floor, exhausted.

Gary teases, "That was fun— let's do it again."

"All righty," Jennifer says.

DEBBY AND GARY

Gary gives the choreographer one of his you-gotta-be-kidding looks, then gets up and dances with just as much energy as he did the first time. Gary says, "I enjoy dancing so much, have such a love for it. It is not something I have to do. It is something I want to do. Doing it makes me happy.

"Jennifer is always smiling and joking. That's wonderful. When other choreographers yell about what's going on, look 'evil,' or don't show respect for the dancers, I am immediately turned off."

Debby is having fun too. "I was a gymnast. I like to move fast. I like to dance with the men. That's a challenge for me. They are known to be stronger, to jump higher, to run faster. In my family I'm an only girl with two brothers. That must have something to do with it.

"I hold a lot of things inside me that I can get out by dancing."

Gary says, "The hardest thing for me in this ballet is the breathing. There is a lot of running. Even though I'm always physical when dancing, I use different muscles and breathing patterns. I was running and holding my breath, which felt stiff. Meanwhile Jennifer kept saying how relaxed so much of this is. I was not relaxed.

"I went home and stood in front of a mirror and asked myself, What did she mean? I thought, I have to remember to breathe while running. Today I tried to loosen up. I kept thinking, There's nothing to it . . . just go ahead and casually do it."

Debora was born in Germany and raised in Philadelphia. "I'm a service brat. My parents were strict; therefore I did not go out much. Everybody's mother and father let their kids take dance class. And so did mine. That was my only outlet at first. Once I was on my own, I gave up dance. I became a potter—but life without dance became boring. I returned to it.

"When I dance, I can get away from myself. I become other people—people that I already am but don't let out in everyday life.

"Jennifer's movement is different from what I'm used to doing in Alvin's work. It is a lot freer. More 'down to the ground.' We are so used to taking ballet classes and being told to pull up. Now we are told to just relax and let it all go.

"It doesn't confuse me, but I've trained my body to feel a certain way. Now I have to untrain it and add something else. It is new, but I like the challenge."

Thursday, July 25: Alvin Ailey comes to the morning's rehearsal carrying a huge pile of books about Australia. He places them on the piano and suggests that the dancers look through them in preparation for the tour. On their "five," most do.

The last section of the ballet to be taught is a series of solos, each with its own theme. Jennifer tells the dancers that they must get to fixed points by certain times in the solos—but between those points they are free to interpret her steps.

Ange says, "Each person has a different sense of rhythm inside. That's what makes modern dance so interesting."

During each solo a group of dancers performs as a chorus by dancing a sequence at another area of the stage. As in "Opening Lines," when "Change" is yelled all of the dancers race from the stage, and another set of dancers picks up where the first group left off.

Jennifer explains "Multiples" as "making soup." Each sequence is a spice or an ingredient. To demonstrate this correctly in this first rehearsal, she has invited two more members of her company, Jennifer Brilliant and Jan Leys. Jennifer, Ange, and Christopher take turns teaching new sequences while Jennifer Brilliant and Jan lead the class. As soon as a step is taught, two dancers at a time dance across the floor, just as in a typical dance class.

Jennifer sings "Te-te-ta" for each pair. She runs through three new sequences. The dancers pick it up almost before she finishes describing the steps. Everyone is in high spirits about finishing the last section of the ballet.

46

"MULTIPLES"

Christopher leaps in to relieve the choreographer. He chants, "Jump—hip, and hip, and hip. . . . The first step is just like the one before the other one . . . AND . . . a very open *arabesque.* Hip way out very open, chest way up to the ceiling, one step in between, jump, land, jump. Hup . . . hup . . . hup. . . .''

Ange teaches another sequence. "This one goes walk, run, and up-hey, and take off with both feet."

Before Ange finishes her directions, Jennifer interrupts, "Okay, let's see it." The company roars with laughter at the impossibility.

Ange tries hard to be serious. She rolls her eyes at Jennifer. "We go *plié* and diagonal, WAMP." She does a jump, trying not to laugh.

Jennifer says, "This jump is with the body straight up and then we have . . ." and she does a very beautiful twisting motion.

"Oh boy," says Gary.

Debby smacks her thigh. "That is nice."

The dancers do the new sequence two at a time. They're off— flying across the floor. Jennifer sings along in the private language that the dancers fully understand. "Bop-bop-bop it's wha-pa-pay, good! Geeeoooorggggeous . . . two, three, four, five, hey." The dancers appear to have mastered the basics of the new routine.

Then Ange jumps in to teach another one. "And it's ONE, two, three, down, hop, slush, slush up, slush, slush up, slush hup, hup . . ." The dancers move fast—so fast that a few of them get tangled up with one another.

Jennifer laughs. "Just when you thought you had it!" Ange goes through the sequence once more. This time they get it right.

Finally Jennifer sets up one more sequence, the click line. "From downstage over here, we start with Ralph, followed by Neisha, then Chaya, Gary, Debora, and Jonathan. This is a fun thing to do; it really is." The dancers go across the stage snapping their fingers. Halfway through they stop and race off. Everybody agrees with Jennifer. They like this.

During the clicks Elizabeth comes out and dances a dazzling solo that was taught during an earlier rehearsal. She runs off, breathless. Oh-oh, she forgot something. She yells "Change!" while sitting down under the *barre*, panting.

Once all the sequences are learned, Jennifer starts to put "Multiples" together. She takes Renee to the far end of the studio. "You will begin here." Then she shows the other dancers where they will be on the stage.

They dance the entire section. When Ralph shouts "Change," they all race off the stage. Jennifer has been racing too, to finish by one o'clock.

48

Neisha says, "I love it. I love it. It has a lot of fun qualities. Soft, slow, speedy."

"That's it, everybody. The steps, the phrases, and the sequences," says Jennifer. They applaud, and she presses the palms of her hands together below her smiling face and bows, Indian style.

ELIZABETH

3. FOCUS

Monday, July 29: Jonathan says, "Dancers bring life to the dreams of the choreographer. We invite the audience to join us in this person's dream. We want to take them there, wherever it is. Every time I see 'Slow Duet' with Danny and Renee, I fall in love. With anyone, everyone. That feeling is so intense. That's part of what we're doing. That's part of the feeling we have up here."

Jennifer explains, "I choreographed *Speeds* in '74, during my last six months as associate artistic director of the Louis Falco Dance Company.

"The word *change* was used onstage as a timing cue—it allowed us to hold the dance together without music. After a while, *change* had a much greater, deeper significance. Not only was there a big change in my life, because it was the year I left Louis and started my own company, but it also came to represent what dance is all about. Dance is change. We're never in one shape for more than a moment. Just as a sculptor changes a plastic form, we dancers change our own bodies. And life is change. No second can replace the next second or the last one."

Jennifer, Ange, and Christopher are eager to get the dancers over the exhaustion of doing the steps. When the timings, the spacings, and all the mechanical aspects are mastered, the dancers will be free to absorb the full impact of the piece, to embrace the non-

ELIZABETH, JENNIFER, AND DEBORA

concrete aspects of dance—what Jennifer calls "the mysterious realm."

Up to this point the dancers have prepared their bodies as instruments, just as a painter prepares paints and brushes. Now comes the interpretation. They begin to look at the movements not only from the outside in, via the mirrors, but from the inside out, via inner feelings and experiences.

Each dancer's approach is different. Before Ralph joined the Ailey company, he danced in Broadway shows, including *A Chorus Line*. He says, "I'm acting as I'm dancing. For me, dance is the art of saying something without saying anything." To do this, Ralph perceives himself in a disembodied or astral condition.

So far Ralph has worked out only the beginning of his role. "During my turns, I'm changing colors. I start off white and beam up. Then there's a glow, a force field. Light comes through my hands and shoots out a cold blue. While I dance, I turn purple, then orange, and then peach. My final jump turns me purple again and back to white. When I walk around the other dancers, rainbow prisms follow my motion."

Early in the ballet Ralph has a series of solo moves where he jumps and turns and races across the stage. "I try to get higher and higher. I have this thing about flying. When I was little I wanted to fly like Peter Pan. I used to jump on my bed to imitate him. When I learned how to jump, it felt like I was flying. I try to stay up as long as I can. When I'm up there, I can look around. It's like going through the clouds in an airplane."

When Carl dances Ralph's part in the same solo, he flies in a different way. His images are not the same. "I like to think that I'm running in air. Sometimes I feel like a bird when I'm dancing. In this piece I shoot across the stage like the comic book character Flash. I can feel the wind behind me when I'm dancing. When I stop, it catches up with me, and then I go again. I'm playing with the wind while I'm playing with the audience."

Jennifer tells the dancers to look around and to react to one another. Gary is trying to figure out whom he should focus on—and when.

He asks himself, "What is 'Trio' all about? Is it an intimate relationship that I have with the two women? Are we just good friends? I think we're three friends having a good time. We look like we're playing games such as leapfrog. Do I like one girl better than the other? I'm beginning to explore those questions."

These dancers are never not working. To develop as artists, it is not enough just to dance. Ange explains, "Jennifer talks about making all this movement feel as if it's inside our own skins. It is not removed from who we are as persons. To reach this point takes time and work. Dancers must look into themselves. To dance who you are, you must first *know* who you are."

Carl

Renee says, "I'm an extremely moody person. I love music that changes drastically because that's me. I love art. I find that going to museums helps me understand the different shapes I make as a dancer. When I'm looking at a painting or a piece of sculpture, I think about its relationship to my body and how it moves me. Because this company does many 'people pieces,' I watch people. Somehow it all ties into my dancing."

Renee and Elizabeth are roommates when the company is on tour. They have similar interests and often visit museums together on their day off. Renee says, "Sometimes I'll look at a painting and say, 'Doesn't this remind you of such-and-such ballet?' Or if Elizabeth and I are learning a new dance, I'll look for a connection with a sculpture, perhaps a similar movement or a similar feeling."

When Elizabeth dances "Slow Duet," there is a moment when the man and the woman lean close to each other and then embrace. "I think of certain paintings by Gustav Klimt. This duet reminds me of him. Everything is so round, so sensuous, and yet so strong."

One of the dancers came to Ange a few days ago and told her that when he was sitting down while working on his VCR, he found himself in the squatting position that is in one of the sections he dances. He thought, *Ah-ha!*

"Those are important moments," says Ange. "Jennifer talks about getting comfortable. Just feel the shape, be in it. Those slight awarenesses let us do just that."

Tuesday, July 30: While the dancers explore the emotional elements of their roles, Jennifer polishes and reviews various sections of the ballet. Sometimes other choreographers and friends poke their heads in to see how things are going. Judith Jamison, the famous Ailey dancer/choreographer, stops by for a "look-see." Jan Leys drops by and is enlisted to demonstrate the refinements of a complicated lift.

ELIZABETH

Jennifer and Jan dance. They are followed by Danny and Renee, then Gary and Elizabeth. The lift does not feel right to Renee, but she and Danny cannot figure out what is wrong. Jennifer takes Renee's part and has Danny lift her so that she can feel how he has been holding Renee. This helps her make a few adjustments to his hand placement.

All three couples dance together. "Don't let your *arabesque* get behind you. . . . THAT'S IT. . . . THAT'S WONDERFUL. . . . MAKE SENSE?" asks Jennifer.

"Yes," says Renee, and she breathes a long, low sigh of relief.

During the second hour of the rehearsal, Alvin Ailey, his associate artistic director, Mary Barnett, and various other members of the company stand by the door watching. Jennifer has the dancers do one full section of the ballet, the last part called "Coda/Folk Dance."

The dancers set very high standards for themselves. They do not like to mess up, even if it is a first run. Renee quickly becomes impatient. "I want something to work, maybe not now but definitely tomorrow. And if it doesn't work by the day after tomorrow, I am upset."

Throughout the run various dancers sing out "Sorry" if they miss a cue or bump into a colleague. Little misses during this rehearsal are not very important. What is important is that all the pieces of the puzzle are beginning to take shape. The tempo has been increased to performance level.

As the dancers move from one sequence to another, Jennifer asks, "Shall we push on? Shall we continue?"

"Yes!" mingles with dancing, breathing, and shouts of "Change!"

Dancers sometimes need to get away from the dance world in order to relieve the pressure. Ruthlyn has two roommates. "They're not dancers, thank goodness. I'm the only one who complains. And they listen. We do many things together when I'm not on tour, including dinners at our house. There's a great amount of record buying and music playing. I like loud music because it's a total escape for me. I'm on the phone for hours.

"I need my life outside to get my head together before I enter the rehearsal room. If my head isn't together, I'll get trampled. The other world out there makes me more confident as a dancer. I know that I'm cared for by my family and friends. I need that."

One lesson aspiring dancers learn when turning professional is that being talented and disciplined is not enough. They have to be aggressive and competitive. Understanding company politics is essential—even in a company that is quite supportive.

There are times when the competition both with oneself and with other dancers can become overwhelming, as Elizabeth Roxas knows. She has been dancing professionally since she was ten years old. "In the Philippines," she says, "everything was handed to me." Once she moved to the States, she realized she had to be more than good. "I did not realize how competitive it was. I had to become pushy. I wasn't one for that." She stopped dancing, moved to Virginia, and became a secretary.

"After a short while away from it, I said no, I can't live this way. I have to go back to dance."

This company is like a close family. On occasion they may differ, squabble, and complain. But they are caring and dependent upon one another. Thirty dancers are constantly working together under pressure. Some are bound not to get along well with others, but when it is time to perform, differences are forgotten. Chaya says, "This company is the best place one could be. If somebody has a problem, right away there are other dancers to help."

Carl agrees. "When we hit the stage, trivial things are left in the dressing room. I may have an argument with someone before a performance. We will go onstage and dance together. Usually when we come off, we both say, 'That was good.' That spat we had before we went on is no longer important."

"What is our impulse to dance?" Christopher asks. "I'm not sure. I think we have things inside of us that we want to share with the world. We want to show the world who we are."

MELINDA, RUTHLYN, AND NEISHA

4. IT ONLY HURTS WHEN I MOVE

Wednesday, *July 31:* Jennifer and Christopher are huddled together going over a new list. In an earlier rehearsal Debby sprained her foot by not doing a *plié* after a high jump. At the end of this week, the doctor will tell her how much healing time she will need. To be able to run the ballet in the next weeks and to ensure that the part is covered, Ruthlyn has been put into "Trio." Today's rehearsal is devoted to bringing her up to the level of the other two.

Gary picks up Ruthlyn and begins spinning her. He yells "WHEEEEEEEE. . . ."

He says, "Debby's accident is a downer, a downer. We went to her home in the Bronx to see her. She won't come to the studio. She's upset. This would have been our first real trio together, and we were excited. We were giggling and laughing as we danced. But Debora and I have to press on.

"Ruthlyn is new. As her partner, it is my job to let her know she can trust me. I tease her and say, 'Don't worry about it. If you make a mistake, I'll fix it.' I'm roughing her up, so to speak."

Because Ruthlyn has never actually danced "Trio," her body doesn't have a clear record of it. Ruthlyn says, "There has to be muscle memory, especially in lifts: when to take off, where my partner is going to place me. At first I watched what Debby was doing and practiced off to the side. I could only pretend to do the

RUTHLYN

lifts, but I tried to understand every detail, such as where she put her foot when she was lifted. Once I understood that and did it several times with Gary, I looked at 'Trio' as an entire section. Only then could I begin creating the mood needed to perform it."

Debora leans forward with her hands on her knees. She braces herself for Ruthlyn to leap onto her back. Gary assists by holding Ruthlyn's arm tightly. She runs, jumps, and misses.

"Embarrassing!" Ruthlyn says, blushing as she checks to make sure she did not hurt Debora.

Gary counsels Ruthlyn. "I'm going to put my hand under your arm, and I'm expecting you to jump on Debora after one—two—three—*glissade* and UP." They try the sequence once again and get it right.

Surprisingly, Ruthlyn is not one bit nervous. "Nervousness is a waste of time. What I want to do is get this learning process over because I'm going to *do* it!" One thing that professional dancers have in common is the ability to work flawlessly under pressure. They never cave in; they blossom.

When a dancer messes up, it may cause another dancer problems. In "Trio" all three dancers jump, kick, and duck. Ruthlyn could easily hurt somebody if she does not know her part perfectly. "I try to zap right into the character. I have to; that's part of a dancer's strength."

The three dancers go over "Trio" until it is second nature to them. Once that happens, the music makes their bodies move. It no longer goes through their heads.

Ruthlyn may have to dance Debby's part in *Elephant* too. "When pressure builds, I keep my wits about me by staying on the lighter side of things.

"My first training was in ballet. Then my interest in dance stopped. I went into sports, such as handball. I even played football. I was a brutal kid. When I returned to the dance, I went to the Ailey school. Here I received training in many techniques: Horton, modern, ballet. I was comfortable with all of it."

Ruthlyn is dealing with an injury herself, tendinitis in her foot. Although she knows that she must be careful, she says, "When I have my time onstage, I'll forget about my injury. I'm going to *live*. I'm going to do my *best*. My foot will hurt, but my confidence is going to be way up there."

During another rehearsal Renee felt sick. She would dance a little, then run off to the women's room. Jennifer sent her home to rest.

Dancers strive to perform during the dance season. Unless an illness has knocked her off her feet, Renee says, "I'll go offstage, get sick, cry, then wipe my face and go back onstage. That's difficult. Sometimes before the performance starts, I don't think I'm going to make it. But I do. It's mind over matter." A dancer does not like to miss a rehearsal and absolutely hates to miss a performance.

Debora often thinks about what she puts her body through. "As I get older, my body changes. I have to keep readjusting to what is happening to it. Some days I wake up and I can't move, but I know I must. I take two aspirins and sit in my tub with the shower on. I'm healthy and strong, but an injury can wipe a dancer out."

"My body is my instrument," says Danny. "I try to respect it by caring for it."

The second hour, Jennifer announces that they will run through the middle, or belly, of the ballet without pausing: from "Trio" to "Fast Duets." Although Marilyn and Jonathan have often practiced "Fast Duets" in the corner, no one in the company has seen them dance the entire piece. Christopher and Ange taught it to them in private evening rehearsals.

"It was their part," says Jonathan. "Originally Jennifer and Louis Falco danced 'Fast Duets.' They taught it to Christopher and Ange, who taught Marilyn and me. There is a real history here.

"The duet is about a race. Who will take off first? The music starts and we don't dance. Tension builds. Then we go. Once we are dancing, we have to catch up to the music. There's a lot of play that way. Christopher and Ange want us to keep the audience and each other in suspense."

Marilyn is enthusiastic too. "It is lovely. Our lines must be clean. The figures must form the same shapes." The choreographer tells them to think of themselves as identical, like a pair of bookends.

Jonathan and Marilyn will become "bookends" by doing their duet in performance, over and over again. Before and after every performance they plan to talk about what they are going to do and who's going to give which cue.

The other dancers applaud wildly as they watch this three-section duet—each part danced faster and faster.

By the end of "Fast Duets," Marilyn and Jonathan are in a sweat and breathless. Jonathan says, "Partnering is my own personal love. Dancing with Marilyn is sensational. I love this piece. It is challenging and beautiful." He curls up by the piano to rest. Ange hunkers down to critique his performance. Even though he is drained, he is eager for Ange's reactions.

Marilyn is pleased. "Jonathan is like energy, pure energy. I'm that way too. We feel each other, and that is wonderful, just wonderful. I like dancing with Jonathan. He's right there."

Marilyn says, "I never thought I would be a dancer, never. I played double-dutch and stickball in my neighborhood in Brooklyn. My girlfriend danced, and I would go with her and watch. She said, 'Why don't you audition with me?' I said no. I'd never even had a class. One day she loaned me her leotards. I put them on and auditioned for a scholarship at the Alvin Ailey school. I got it; she didn't. I wanted to give the scholarship to her, but she wouldn't take it. I went to the school for four years. Now here I am, the senior female dancer of the company."

Elizabeth dances a striking solo publicly for the first time. When the alternates run through the belly of the ballet, Ruthlyn dances the same solo. She brings a different sensibility to the shapes. Both dancers have long graceful limbs. When they go into an extension, raising and holding a leg in the air above shoulder level, their ballet training becomes apparent.

Everyone is fascinated to see how the variations come together and intertwine. Gary is overjoyed. "At last!" he says, and falls down, exhausted.

DEBORA

5. THE RUN-THROUGHS

*T*hursday, *August 1:* Jennifer announces the first full run-through of *Speeds.* "A run-through?" Ruthlyn screams as she clutches Gary's jacket. "Do I know this?"

"I'll make you know it!" Gary assures her.

Renee says, "Sometimes it is hard to perform in front of the company. They are much more critical than the audience. They see no makeup, no costumes, no lights. On top of that, sometimes you're doing exactly what they wanted to do."

The dancers have been separated into smaller groups to learn various parts of the dance. Even though they see each other every day—falling down and looking funny—there is still a touch of nervousness the first time they dance a new work for their peers.

Other people begin to arrive: Alvin Ailey, Mary Barnett, Keith Simmons, Susan Hilferty, a few friends of Jennifer's, and Tim Hunter, the company lighting designer.

Lighting designers work in many different ways. Tim always begins by watching a rehearsal. "I start by watching the choreographer's forms and movement. Then I work at making my own statement. When I get ideas, I sketch angles of light with a white pencil on a black piece of paper."

ANGE, CHRISTOPHER, ALVIN AILEY, AND MARILYN

The spectators take their places on the benches in front of the mirrored wall. Ange and Christopher prepare to take notes of the corrections that Jennifer will whisper to them while the dancers run through the ballet. The dancers begin.

Even this small audience makes Danny anxious. "It's bad, but it's good. It is bad in that I don't feel free enough to make mistakes, because they are watching. They want a finished product and I don't have one yet. On the other hand, I can try my interpretations on them. I hope I sense a reaction. If they react positively, I feel good. They're not going to applaud, or maybe they will." They do, a number of times.

Danny says, "I don't see the audience while I'm dancing, but I can feel them. If a dancer is boring, the audience fidgets. If a dancer is captivating, they are glued."

Christopher says that when the link has not been fully made between the dancer and the role, the audience will experience a subtle, perhaps indescribable discomfort. Or they will ask: *Why?* What was that about? What were they trying to express?

After the finale there is loud applause. People congratulate the dancers with smiles so big that one would think it was opening night. Elizabeth says, "I was nervous. I wasn't sure I could do it the right way. Everybody was there, and that's hard. Once I got past that first entrance and began to dance, it felt right."

Alvin Ailey embraces his dancers. Jennifer, jubilant, talks with the visitors. The dancers collapse.

During the run Carl sat by a window under the *barre* watching intently. "I'm not going to lie. Sometimes I get envious watching Ralph do the part. On the other hand, I like Ralph. I enjoy watching him dance. And he enjoys watching me. We talk about our role and support each other."

Friday, August 2: Ange and Christopher gather the group into a circle and go over the previous day's notes. Ange says that she wishes she hadn't had to take notes because she wanted to savor every little moment. "I was very, very impressed. *Speeds* is a

ANGE GIVES NOTES

tough ballet. Everybody is out there dancing all the time. It feels mammoth."

From age four Ange knew she would become a dancer. "Mom wanted to be a dancer, but she went the traditional route. She married and had children. Dance was a leftover dream for her. I just happened to love her dream.

"I went to boarding school at Interlochen Arts Academy in Michigan and then majored in dance at Juilliard. During my senior year one of my teachers told me that Louis Falco was holding a women's audition. I didn't know who he was, but I was determined to find out what auditioning was all about.

"It was very well organized. Falco sat next to Jennifer and his entire company behind a long table. Burt Alcantara played the drums. One hundred fifty women showed up to audition. I have an aggressive streak in me that comes out when I dance. I was determined to do better than all of the others. They began by teaching us a few phrases. I *worked!*

"I could tell that Jennifer wanted me. Still, I had to go through six more auditions before they said yes. From the very first day Jennifer was an amazing person in my life. When she formed her own company, I went with her."

Chaya says, "It is important for all the dancers to continue dancing the ballet from top to bottom. Jennifer is giving us a chance to do that. We must get the feeling of the entire piece, not just section by section. There are still layers to explore."

Jennifer is called to her studio. She asks Ange and Christopher to do the run. They are excited. They've never conducted a company run. Just as they are about to begin, Alvin Ailey walks into the studio with Roland Petit, the famous French choreographer. They have come to see the run-through. Ange gulps and looks at Christopher. He seems to hesitate, then takes a deep breath and walks to the center of the studio. Poised, he says, "Shall we begin?" The dancers respond to their friend's uneasy position by dancing a great run-through.

When Christopher was a child in Detroit, he went to acting school. He also painted. By age thirteen his interest in the visual arts waned. He took his first dance class about that time. He evolved into a dancer without leaving painting behind. Christopher says, "Dancing is like drawing with your whole body. Painting and dancing have similar physical sensations. The motions that I make with my hand when I'm drawing are in many ways similar to the motions I make when I'm dancing—the up, down, around, the swoop, the corner, the diagonal, the straight line, the bumpy line, the smooth line."

During the second hour of rehearsal, the visitors are gone. Ange and Christopher read more notes. Notes deal with broad themes: where the dancers must focus; their use of the space. Notes are also about details: "The *arabesque* needs to be turned a touch to the right"; "The arms are in second position."
Jonathan complains that it did not go well for him. He bumped

68

JENNIFER AND ANGE

into people twice. He wasn't sufficiently warmed up. And so on. Dancers are their own worst critics.

While the note session takes place, Susan and Connie enter with costumes under their arms. They want Renee to try a skirt. They scrutinize her as she gracefully moves into a *penchée.*

Alvin Ailey returns. The look on his face shows his pride as he announces that the People's Republic of China has invited the company to perform after the Australia tour. It is the first American modern dance company invited to China since diplomatic relations were established with the United States! The dancers are pleased.

Debora says that Ailey's visits make rehearsals more fun for her. "Often he brings *everybody* in from the school." She laughs. "He must walk through the halls gathering students who don't have class. 'What are you doing?' 'Nothing.' 'Come on and see my dancers.' He's proud of us.

"When he's here watching, I dance better, perhaps because of the way I feel about him. If I didn't have any personal feelings for him, then I would be very uptight because he is *Alvin Ailey*. But by working with him, I have seen the private side of him. He is caring and sensitive. I value his comments."

Monday, August 5: Debby arrives wearing an elastic bandage on her left foot. Jennifer hugs her and says, "You must promise me that today you will only walk it through. I want you to rest."

Before she can reply, Mary Barnett rushes into the studio to see Debby. "No hard dancing, do you hear?" she admonishes.

Debby says, "I promise."

Mary smiles, shaking her head. She knows Debby only too well. "My foot feels better," Debby tells them. "It was just a sprain."

Everyone is glad to see Debby. Ruthlyn gives her a big hug. No one knows who will dance "Trio." For Debby, though, it is certain. Ruthlyn continues to rehearse. She may not dance *Speeds* in Washington, but she knows she will perform it in Australia.

Debby has been with the company for five years. She started dancing in Philadelphia at the age of three. "Mine is the usual story of a mother putting her daughter into dancing school for the discipline and physical beauty of the dance. I used to perform at home when I was little. I had those little gym suits, the blue ones with the belt. I would put one on along with one of my mother's wigs, high-heeled shoes, and makeup. As soon as she came in the door, I would have her sit down and watch a little dance routine. She always did. My mother is my dearest fan. All of my family is very supportive. When I danced with Philadanco, if no one else was in the audience when we performed, we could always count on three people: my mother, my grandmother, and my aunt. They came to every show. At one point they knew all the steps."

As the rehearsal ends, Jennifer takes a moment to talk about her ballet. "*Speeds* is about celebration. It is about fun. It's a friendly piece."

Chaya asks, "Does it look like we're playing a game?"

"Absolutely! As it should," replies Jennifer. "Of course, there's the romantic part; there's the delicate part; there's the crash part.

"When my company does it, there are times when we go in the wrong direction. We start to make little personal jokes. That's out. That's wrong." Everyone laughs. "As you are dancing, you can notice the other people. Look at each other. Let your personalities come out. What I don't want to see is for you to suddenly become 'dancers.' That's not *Speeds*. *Speeds* is you, as you see yourselves. Alone, together, dancing."

Upstairs in the Ailey executive offices, Bill Hammond is on a transatlantic telephone call. "My dancers must have one full day off each week." He is calm, smiling, but very firm. "No, a travel day does not count as a day off."

Next door Adrienne Warren, the publicity director, is going over contact sheets of head photographs for the programs in Australia. Telephones ring off the hooks while dancers pop in to see photographs.

A publicity director is the person who provides information to the press. Adrienne writes the program copy as well as the press releases. She follows up on hundreds of details to give the public information about the company.

Adrienne was a dancer in her hometown, Detroit. She stopped when her body started to hurt. "I wasn't willing to make the sacrifice to become the ultimate dancer. I wanted to be on the business end of it. I liked the idea of putting on a suit and carrying an attaché case."

Across the hall in the conference room, three costume designers are collecting and fitting costumes for the three new ballets.

71

Tuesday, August 6: Keith makes a few announcements. "As of tomorrow all rehearsals will take place at Manhattan Community College. I'll have directions typed for you. Also you should know that you go directly from Wolf Trap to the tour of Australia and China. Be packed for the tour."

Jennifer steps in to announce, "I have named Chaya and Gary the official rehearsal directors." A rehearsal director rehearses the ballet when the company is on tour and the choreographer is unavailable. Directors must know the ballet as well as the dancers and choreographer do. It helps when they themselves have danced in it.

The group is delighted with Jennifer's decision. They break into wild applause. "Bravo—bravo—bravo!" "Hurray—hurray!"

Wednesday, August 7: Susan arrives with a long metal rack stuffed with clothing. She has a costume list for each dancer, and each costume on the rack is labeled.

FINDING COSTUMES

Neisha

Today's rehearsal is aimed at working out the many rapid costume changes. The costumes must be stored on the right or left side of the stage, according to the dancers' entrances and exits.

Jonathan zips up a spiffy white jumpsuit that he will wear in "Fast Duets." He turns up his collar and rolls up his sleeves. "This suit is perfect for my movement," he shouts. He rushes over to show Alvin Ailey.

The dancers walk around admiring one another's costumes. Ruthlyn adores the flowing shirt Elizabeth will wear for her solo. "And Danny, that tuxedo shirt for 'Slow Duet' . . . you look fabulous." Danny likes it, too.

The costumes are not finished. There are seams to be sewn and material to be taken in. Susan doubts that dancers should dance with pins in their clothing. Jennifer agrees. "I think it's a little dangerous. I'd rather they look baggy."

There's one problem. Ralph is not happy with his costume. In his opening solo he wears overalls with white cotton ties on the shoulders and the legs. Susan can't get him to tie the bottom ties. She wonders why he is struggling. Is it vanity or has it

ELIZABETH AND SUSAN

something to do with the movement? She watches him dance and realizes that his movement is sleek and angular. With the pants tied off at the ankles, the movement becomes much rounder. Instead of enhancing Ralph's angularity, her costume is fighting it.

After the rehearsal Susan narrows Ralph's pant legs and removes the ties. Now his appearance meshes with his interpretation of the role.

When the dancers do the first run-through in costume, they look at one another as they dance. They smile as each new dancer makes an entrance and cannot restrain laughter when Marilyn grandly dances out in weird striped glasses. Even though the dancers are tired from the long, exhausting hours, they are having fun.

MARILYN

ELIZABETH

Elizabeth dances her solo in costume. As she dances, her colleagues marvel at her graceful line. But a perfect line is not all that counts for Elizabeth. "In order to become an artist, not just a dancer, one must not worry about technique all the time. What is inside the dancer is what counts. That is the difference between being just a plain performer and being an artist."

At the end of the rehearsal, Jennifer thanks the company. They applaud her. It is Wednesday. There are only three rehearsal days left in New York. Everyone is very tired. Everything hurts. Fortunately, Jonathan gives great massages. The dancers line up for them. They take a lunch break or a nap before going off to other rehearsals. Jennifer, Ange, and Christopher return to their studio to work with their own company.

Later that evening Christopher meets Chaya for a private rehearsal. They concentrate on every gesture. Chaya says, "The most difficult thing for me is incorporating a new choreographer's style into my own way of moving.

"What is the actual meaning of Jennifer's style? My body does it, but my head does not. In so many places I have too much control. My body doesn't go suddenly relaxed. I'm stubborn.

"Christopher has me dance a shape and then asks, 'How do you feel?' I say, 'Very uncomfortable,' because I am not used to the shape. Then Christopher says, 'Try to slow down and remember that uncomfortable feeling. Relax your body. Work from the feeling. Then it becomes comfortable.' Now it feels good. When something excites me or when my concentration is off, I go back to my old way.

"I must always be relaxed. How can I do that? In my imagination first. I picture the studio as a crystal ball. Second, I see Christopher wearing his red shirt or jogging pants. He's showing me a movement. And third, I see Jennifer in her black outfit going, 'Haaaaa.' That brings me back to a relaxed state.

"I was thinking about that all last weekend. I went to a friend's beach house. I have a tape of the *Speeds* music. While I was lying out on the deck, I was thinking, thinking, thinking."

ANGE AND ELIZABETH

6. TECHNICAL REHEARSALS

Wednesday, August 7: Ange and Christopher are polishing movements with the two "Trio" casts. No longer are the dancers in their elegant, airy, familiar studio with the long wall-to-wall mirrors where they can check an *arabesque* or Jennifer's deep *pliés.* At Manhattan Community College they must rely on their instincts, their training, their teachers, and one another.

Looking in a mirror is a very mechanical act that lets dancers see the shapes of their bodies and make outward adjustments. But it doesn't help them feel the movements—and onstage they will be on their own.

Elizabeth says, "It's scary without the mirror. I don't have the security that I have when I see myself. I can only judge my performance from inside and what I sense from the audience. The audience becomes my mirror."

Ange works with the "Trio" alternates. She reminds them to look at one another as they dance. Carl creeps toward Neisha. He moves his fingers as if hypnotizing her. Neisha reacts with a startled, fluttery smile. "Good reaction, Neish," says Ange, applauding.

Marilyn, Neisha, and Carl dance. Debby, once again scheduled to dance opening night, sits on the sideline carefully taping her sore foot. Christopher comforts her by rubbing her back. Gary lies on a long bare table, stretching, resting. Debora studies the alternates as they run through "Trio." Everyone is utterly exhausted.

The "Trio" dancers take a break while Ange works with Elizabeth's solo. Ange asks Elizabeth how she feels when she makes her entrance. Elizabeth thinks about it for a moment and says, "Because I enter near the end of 'Slow Duet,' the music makes me feel as if I'm running into a forest. It is very misty, even mysterious. Though moving very slowly, I'm not sad, but not joyous either."

In her solo Elizabeth jumps, throws back her body, and then turns away. "Ange and I figure out how my feelings can best be projected out front. I must pay attention to every nuance: how my face looks, how I smile."

Another movement calls for Elizabeth to look at the audience over her shoulder. Ange interprets this as sharing a secret with the audience. Elizabeth can use Ange's idea to interpret the same movement. With great patience Elizabeth works on imparting meaning to what seems a simple look.

After a lunch break the dancers meet in the college's main theater for the full technical rehearsal. But first Jennifer rehearses the onstage spacing to make sure the dancers know where to be at each moment in the ballet. Stages are divided into five panels. An X, called a spike mark, designates the center and marks off the quarter sections of the stage. Sometimes a spike mark is placed where a major duet or solo is to begin. Dancers know roughly where they must move. But every theater has different dimensions that affect positioning. A dancer's instincts must be refined for each stage.

Jennifer begins by rehearsing the opening walk. Chaya leads the dancers as they snake around the stage. The tempo changes in this walk create different atmospheres. The first part has an

NEISHA, JONATHAN, DEBBY, GARY, RALPH, MARILYN

elegant, romantic gait. As Chaya reaches the middle panel, the tempo gradually changes. The walk becomes relaxed, a casual stride. Finally, as he leads the group toward the rear, they begin a Charlie Chaplinesque run and leave the stage.

"It is coming along," says the choreographer as the dancers gather around her.

They move on to the next sequence in "Opening Lines," called "eights, sixes, fours." The dancers must walk forward in a perfectly straight line without looking at one another. There is no music to help them count tempo. This makes the opening more difficult than it may appear.

The lines are not even. The dancers do it once more. Elizabeth tries to lift everyone's spirits. In a deep, heavy voice she groans,

"Change." Other dancers pick up on that and yell "Change" in funny voices.

Once the company works through all the spacing, they are ready for the first run-through with costumes, music, and the new spacing. "No dancing this time around," Jennifer says. "Take it easy, walk it through." Then she plans to talk about some of the remaining problems. After that, they will dance a run-through "full out."

The dancers are exuberant about dancing *Speeds* in costume on a stage with lights and music. Backstage there is giggling, stretching, and happy chaos. Elizabeth and Renee share a mirror to touch up their makeup. Marilyn is delighted with the large white dangling earrings that Susan found for her first entrance. "It's *showtime*," Debby sings as she carries off her costume.

RENEE AND ELIZABETH

Keith

During the run-throughs Keith will supervise the backstage activities and the onstage performance.

"People often don't understand that my job has artistic qualities. I feel as if I'm performing the ballet along with the dancers. I have the same nervousness as they do. If the lighting or other cues are not all together, it won't look right."

After some last-minute stretches, the first run begins. Although Jennifer has asked for a "marking" run-through, the dancers, inspired by the lights and a real stage, work full out.

Ralph says, "I disappear as a person. I become something else. The audience no longer exists. No one is onstage or even in the wings with me. There is nothing solid. I am in a new place where I can create a story based upon my understanding of the dance."

Christopher is enthralled by what the dancers do with "his" ballet. Each time he sees a run-through, he becomes more pleased, less apprehensive. And Jennifer? The rapt look on her face tells it all.

RENEE AND RALPH

Danny begins the duet. "I think of the nighttime. I see stars. I see moonlight. They combine. That's one of the images I use most. Trying to make my part say something is fun."

Debora glides across the stage. She says, "I like small audiences where I can actually see the people. We're told never to focus down, but I often find myself dancing to the first three rows."

At the end of the performance, Jennifer shouts, *"Wow!* If that's 'marking,' I can't wait to see it full out." People in the audience applaud and shout, "Encore!" "Bravo!" A few performers peek out from the wings and curtsy. The dancers take a break. Jennifer goes backstage to congratulate them.

"Why don't we give ourselves a minute to rest and then do it again?" says Jennifer. She turns to go back to her seat, stops, spins around, and looks at the dancers. What she says is simple, but not many remember to say, "Thank you."

The second run-through begins. As Renee dances "Slow Duet," she asks herself, "Am I reaching for something more tonight?" Each performance is an opportunity for Renee to "reach beyond" realistic expectations. Many dancers share this goal. Sometimes the striving may cause a dancer to overreach and fall. Renee says, "I know I should not fall down. But I test myself to see how far my body can go. I learn by extending myself. Falling is not as embarrassing as one might suppose. In fact, if done because of reaching too far, it feels good."

At the end of a very long day, everyone is wiped out. Neisha says, "I go home at night after the rehearsal, and my back is sore, my feet are killing me, my mind 'needs a break.' I wake up in the morning, and you'd think I was ninety years old because I have to hop to the bathroom to take a hot shower. After that, I'm fine. Sometimes I think, Why am I doing this to myself? I could have been a lawyer. I could have been a doctor. I could have been a typist. . . . But I know that I would not have been happy. That's because deep down inside, I love what I do."

GARY, DEBBY, AND DEBORA

Thursday, August 8: Dancers straggle onto a small stage at the college. There weren't enough hours in the night to sleep away the grueling day they had yesterday. No one sits. Dancers crawl into any position that offers some amount of relief to their muscles. Along with their dance clothing, they carry coffee, vitamins, rubbing creams, ice packs. Carl wears his "funny hat" and two-steps across the stage. Everyone perks up.

Jennifer whisks in, bubbling with excitement. "I want to say that I felt wonderful after last night. I know it was hard to do the two runs. The thing that pleased me most is that everybody's starting to make it their own. Everybody is starting to fly in it. That makes me joyous.

"Another terrific thing about yesterday was the relaxation apparent among you. People are being themselves within the piece."

Jennifer's spontaneous appreciation lifts the dancers' spirits. They pull themselves together to generate the energy needed to begin the rehearsal. Even though the ballet is at performance level, there are still details to work on—over and over again. This two-hour rehearsal is devoted to refining specific movements and to giving the dancers a chance to work on their alternate parts.

"All righty, this is gonna be a little confusing. But it won't be if we figure this out together." Dancers walk to the back of the stage. "Some people from cast A are going to stay in certain parts, but not in others."

Jennifer begins by reading from a long list that she wrote late last night. "In 'Opening Lines,' we trade Gary for Danny, Elizabeth for Renee, Melinda for Neisha, Rodney for John, Debby stays in, Carl for Gary, Debora stays in, Ralph stays in, Marilyn stays in, Ruthlyn for Elizabeth, and Max for Chaya. That's operative for the opening. Right? Click, click, gear, boom! The whole opening through the click line.

"Okay . . . 'Circle Dance' . . ." She continues to read names. At

CARL

one point she tells Carl he will dance both Gary's and Ralph's parts this rehearsal. "You're a Jekyll and Hyde today; you're a split personality." Carl nods. He's ready.

To dance two roles is not an easy task. "Ralph's role is more playful for me," Carl says. "I sparkle. I'm a sparkly person. I'm someone who shimmers all the time. I imagine that I'm a star. When I'm onstage, I twinkle.

"In Gary's role I'm massive. I'm commanding. I manipulate people. Gary is laid back when he dances it, but more powerful.

"Doing both roles isn't physically draining, but mentally it is. I have to be mentally prepared to quickly shift personalities."

Jennifer sings the beats as the dancers move to her tempo. "Hey, you're fast," Gary interrupts while he dances Danny's part.

Jennifer laughs and replies, "That's what it needs." There are sounds of feet moving across the stage. "YOU'VE GOT IT! THAT'S IT!" she shouts.

"Yeah!" agrees Gary.

Gary, who has always seen this ballet as more than his single part, is beginning to ease into his role as rehearsal director. He is asserting himself more and more. He watches the overall shape of the ballet.

Chaya, the codirector, spontaneously concentrates on details. He watches the other dancers and corrects a position or a movement. When he is not dancing, he moves to the side of the stage with a colleague and reviews his or her part.

The two men, Gary and Chaya, complement one another, and though there is a natural impulse to hold on to "their" ballet, the Works people encourage the Ailey dancers to make it their own.

Ange notices that Chaya is upset. When she asks him why, he tells her that Max is having bad pains in his back. Max refuses to tell the front office for fear they will take him out of the new ballets. "I'm all right, I'm all right," Max says. "Nothing serious." He proves it by doing some difficult jumps perfectly. But Ange is worried. So is Jennifer.

The choreographer announces, "First cast." That is one way to get Max to stop dancing. He lies down in the aisle and falls asleep.

After the lunch break the dancers put as much energy into the other new ballets. The schedule of who dances what, when, and where has been made up in the executive offices. Various dancers, choreographers, designers, and stagehands rush about the three rehearsal areas allotted to the company. It is up to Keith to hand out the schedules. Keith remains calm through it all. Everyone looks to him or to the other stage manager, Calvin Hunt, when they want to know what to do or where to go.

MAX AND CHAYA

Friday, August 9: "Everybody onstage," announces Keith. If the dancers thought they were tired before rehearsal yesterday, that was nothing compared to the way they feel today. Jennifer, standing center stage, says, "Let's see our lineup."

As dancers warm up, there is a touch on the leg, a pat on the back, or a smile of encouragement from someone, everyone, anyone. A glance or a giggle can make a big difference.

Everyone senses the need to keep morale up. Jonathan waddles across the stage wearing huge red and green socks, his "funny socks." Everyone notices them and comments on how wonderful they are. He bows and tells the group, "Granny made them."

Jennifer wants everyone to wear white so that Tim can check the lights. Jonathan doesn't want to give up his socks. Jennifer says, "You can keep the socks on, but basically we need to see how the new lighting cues work on those lovely bodies in white clothes." Jonathan, not beyond flattery, is pleased. So are his fellow dancers. Since they are exhausted, even a little praise, however insignificant in normal circumstances, revs up enthusiasm.

Tim checks the lights onstage and goes to his place at the light box in the rear of the orchestra. "I have an assistant and electricians who take care of the technical aspects. That frees me to dream up ideas. They help me figure out how to make my ideas happen.

"It is important to keep the floor lit so the dancers know where they are. It is possible to light a dancer and not light the floor, but if they can't see, they may end up facing the wrong way or falling.

"Jennifer's piece is very geometrical. There are many shapes, forms, and lines that intersect or create diagonals. Alvin's ballets are that way too. *Speeds* fits in well with this company.

"In designing *Speeds*, I didn't work as much with the dancers as I did with the clothes. They are white and pristine. That determined what angles of light and what colors I would use."

In *Speeds* the same colors come from both sides of the stage: a pale blue, a lavender, and a soft amber. Tim would light a piece with more tension differently. He would place different colors on each side of the stage. That heightens contrast on the form of the dancers; the colored shadows bring out the muscular detail.

"Jennifer's piece does not have the look or the feeling of tension. It is wide open, and the dancers, the costumes, and the movement tell the whole story.

"I have to work fast. I only have two hours before the tech rehearsal to set the lights. I like that. I like the pressure. Either I come off looking great, or it all falls in on me. There isn't anything in between. That's one reason I like this job."

Jennifer says, "Today we must do two runs. On the first run some alternates will do the middle of the piece, from 'Trio' through 'Fast Duets.' All alternates should put on something white so that Tim can check his lighting. The first cast should get into their opening outfits."

Elizabeth wants to know how she should wear her hair. Jennifer takes a moment and looks at it. Then she decides, "For 'Slow Duet' you can wear it pulled back, but for your solo I prefer it long and loose." Every little detail must be taken into account.

Keith says, "Stand by, dancers . . . AND curtain . . . GO!"

Carl dances Ralph's solo. He says, "I get nervous before a performance. As soon as the curtain is up, I know that I can give it everything I've got. Some people are shy when they are onstage, but not me. I'm the opposite. I am not a brassy person offstage, but I don't mind opening up onstage. I have no inhibitions there."

During "Multiples," Jonathan bumps into a few people. "That was terrible," he complains. He is tired, but Jennifer isn't worried. She knows he will be great in his part.

Once the run-through is finished, Jennifer joins Christopher at the rear of the orchestra. They give lighting notes to Tim. He must make it clear that colors change every time a dancer says "Change." Tim fine-tunes the timing of the cues, speaking to the

JENNIFER GIVES LIGHTING NOTES TO TIM

electricians through a head microphone. He says such things as "Change cue eighteen to when Gary says 'Change.'"

The first cast begins to dance. All is quiet. Keith calls out the lighting cues as the dancers work through the piece.

Jonathan isn't happy with this performance either. He and Marilyn go off in a corner to plan new strategy. Stagehands are moving lights while dancers are preparing for the next rehearsal.

By this point in the rehearsal process, the dancers are filled with images. The mental images inform the physical placements. The physical placements inform the mental images. These go back and forth as the movements for each dancer evolve. Partners are responding to each other's personal images. A duet develops as they explore each movement individually and together.

JONATHAN AND MARILYN

Jennifer takes time to talk with Renee about the dramatic intent of "Slow Duet." "Jennifer explained how it is possible to make a different emotional statement from movement to movement. An entire dance does not have to stay with one expression," Renee says. "The movement affects the facial expression."

Jennifer suggested that Renee think of each shape as a different part of a love affair. Confidence. Doubt. Passion. Tenderness. Power. Helplessness. Restraint. Wildness.

Renee says, "No one had explained it before in those terms—at least, other explanations had not made as strong an impact. I know I won't have time to fully incorporate what she said until we leave the States.

"After talking with Jennifer, I wanted to let her know how deeply she touched me." It is the end of the week. Renee is exhausted. She looks at Jennifer, puts her arms around her, and bursts into tears. "No words can express what I got from that conversation. The only thing that can is my performance. Still, I wish I could say something—or *do* something—special."

Once the rehearsal ends, Jennifer, Christopher, and Ange meet with Chaya and Gary to go over who will dance the parts on tour. This meeting, in effect, passes *Speeds* from The Works to the Ailey company. Now the ballet is in their hands.

7. ON TOUR

*M*onday, August 12: While waiting for the company bus, Gary says, "I went to California and back by station wagon with my old dance company. There were two station wagons and a truck following with the lights, the floor, and the costumes. We would arrive at a town and have to iron the costumes ourselves. We would put the floor down and the lights up. We would dance the show, take everything down, put it back on the truck, ride to the next place, and start over again. You can be sure it is not like that here. Here we fly everywhere, check into the hotel, are driven to the theater. This is a piece of cake!"

On the shuttle to Washington, D.C., Ange says, "When I dance, I am in control of the ballet. As an assistant to the choreographer, I become a passive participant. *Speeds* belongs to the dancers now. I'm happy. I'm sad. I'm nervous."

Jennifer makes more lists:

1. Meet Chaya and Gary—review casting.
2. Meet Susan—check last-minute costume changes.
3. Grab Tim and Keith about the lighting cues.
4. Ask Keith about digitizing the music tape.
5. Write movement list for the photo session.

Elizabeth says, "Now that the rehearsal period is over, the fun and games are over too. In rehearsals we are performing for ourselves. But onstage our responsibility is to the audience. My new job is to make sure that what I am trying to say, what I have worked on for all these weeks, projects to the audience."

At the theater in Wolf Trap, Virginia, Melinda sits on a couch in the lounge near the dressing rooms. "I am excited," she says. "I was very nervous yesterday. Everybody was saying to me, 'But you're not even dancing.' That didn't help. I was still nervous."

   Debby is pacing back and forth in the dressing room. She is full of energy. "When we rehearse, we do the same thing over and over and over and over. I get tired. Performing is totally different. There is one chance to do it! No matter what happens, we've got to give it our all. I am in a different state of mind when I perform. When I dance, I have no troubles."

DEBORA

Carl says, "Dancing before an audience is like being pulled by magnets. The audience is a magnet and I am a magnet. Onstage I can feel the energy going back and forth, back and forth. It makes me dance harder, more forcefully. At times I've danced with a connection so strong that I go off by myself afterward and cry. That's when I know that I've given everything that I can give.

"At the moment when I know my performance is good, I feel my dancing being taken to another level. People may call it artistry. That tender connection between the performer and the audience is the fulfillment for me."

How to Walk an Elephant premieres opening night at Wolf Trap. The last ballet of the evening is Alvin Ailey's *Revelations.*

Melinda and Ruthlyn watch the dances from the wings. "When we were members of the junior repertory company, we did *Revelations*, but in a slightly different version," says Melinda. "It is *the piece* for the Ailey company. Tonight is the first time I have seen it as a member of the first company. This makes everything real to me."

Jennifer goes backstage to congratulate the choreographers, Bill T. and Arnie. She embraces dancers as they bound up the stairs to the stage door.

"Only two more days," Jennifer says to Debora as they wait for the company bus to take them back to the hotel.

"I can hardly wait to dance *Speeds*," Debora confesses.

Back at the hotel, dancers split up into groups of three and four for late suppers. Jonathan brings pizza back to his hotel room. Marilyn and Ralph? Why, they go dancing!

The Ailey company tours for months at a time. Being on the road regularly is rough. It leaves little time for socializing outside the group. Danny says, "Sometimes I think I would like to settle down and have a relationship. But I'm caught up now. I've put so much energy into dancing—and I really do love it—that I want to see it through.

"When I become more successful, then I'll be able to call the shots, and maybe then I can slow down. Perhaps I could build a normal life, whatever a normal life is."

Jonathan says that his mind, his spirit, and his body are in shock from how hard professional dancing is. "I've discovered that although it is wonderful to see other countries and other peoples, I don't like being away for ten months a year. But by the same token, there is something so special about dancing. My second thoughts stop the minute I step out on that stage. The most important thing in my life right now is nothing other than that moment. The feeling that I get when I am there makes all the hard work, and everything else that goes with dancing, worth it."

Neisha has been engaged to be married for three years. Her fiancé is a professional musician. He, too, travels. Being in the same town together longer than one month is a great event. Why would Neisha put herself through all this work? "When I'm onstage, nobody can touch me. It's my time. I can really express myself."

Tuesday, August 13: The dancers arrive at breakfast refreshed and exhilarated. The waitress comes to the table. "Here's your change," she says.

"Change!" Ruthlyn yells, and she jumps up and goes into a "Jennifer shape." People at other tables turn around. They must think she's loony. She's not loony, she's a dancer.

After breakfast Ralph does his daily *barre* exercises in the swimming pool. The warm water relaxes his tired muscles. First he swims, then stretches, then swims, then stretches.

Jack Mitchell, the famous dance photographer, arrives at Wolf Trap. Dancers in each new ballet are called onstage to be photographed. These photographs will be used for publicity all over the world.

By four-thirty *Speeds* is called. The dancers have been working onstage in makeup and costumes since one o'clock. On top of

CHAYA, GARY, AND DEBORA

that, it's hot—ninety-eight degrees. Yet the dancers must look fresh for Mr. Mitchell's cameras.

Onstage the thick fire curtain is drawn in order to keep out ambient light. Five giant strobes make the stage even hotter.

Jennifer has a list of action shots; the dancers jump, turn, twist, and leap. There isn't much time left. The technicians running the stage lights want to break for dinner. Keith tries to stall them as long as possible.

The photographer checks his lighting. Jennifer stands behind him, calling, "One—two—three . . . WHA-PA." At the "PA," he shoots. Light blasts across the stage. Chaya stands by to fan the dancers, wipe their brows, and give encouragement and cheer. "Great! That was gorgeous!" shouts Jennifer as the dancers jump and smile.

100

Once the session is over, all the dancers return downstairs to their dressing rooms. In the lounge Susan is busy reviewing last-minute details with the costume supervisor, Toni James. All the costumes will be turned over to Toni and her assistant, Anne Payne. They maintain the clothes while the company is on tour.

"I don't get involved with the ballet until it has opened," says Toni. "After that, it is my responsibility to do what is necessary to the clothing, even replace it. I make sure everything is clean and ready for performance. If anyone splits anything, I have to be there to mend it."

As the dancers return their costumes to Toni, Susan watches nearby. "All I can think of are the things that aren't going to get done." There are always pages of notes left. Once a ballet opens, that's it. No changes.

"There's a part of me that can't wait until the company goes off to Australia," Susan continues. "Then there's another part of me that can't believe that they will be separated from me.

"Often I won't go to opening-night parties because they make me feel so melancholy. When the dance opens, my work is over. But for the performer, it is just beginning."

Tim drops by the dressing area to buy a sandwich at the canteen. Tim and his crew need darkness in order to set the lights. Because the theater is "open air," they work all night after each performance.

Tim says, "All the cues are in a computer. Keith says, 'Stand by cue one. . . . Go.' A man hits a button and the computer changes eight hundred dimmers. They all go to different levels. Six hundred lights change intensity. It used to take six or eight people to do that. Big handles. Big contraptions. With the computer the design possibilities are infinite. I can be subtle, then strong; complex, then simple. I can control everything."

Before the evening performance Melinda paces the hall outside the dressing rooms. Tonight is her first performance, the premiere of *Lament.* She says she is nervous. "Fortunately, I'll be wearing a mask."

Wednesday, August 14: It is the day of the *Speeds* premiere. A most important part of the making of a ballet is about to appear: the audience.

11:00: In Jennifer's hotel room, Ange and Christopher wrap bottles of champagne and write personal notes for each member of the cast, alternates, and crew. Jennifer is at the typewriter, typing the order of the final bows.

Downstairs at the swimming pool, dancers stretch, swim, joke, and relax. Jonathan can hardly sit still. "I am more excited about this ballet than almost any other thing I've been in," he says. "Ralph is my roommate when we are on tour. He has made up an entire story line for his role. He's so advanced. I learn so much from him. But I don't take the story line approach; I interpret my part in this ballet as me—Jonathan—doing a dance that I love."

The sense of obligation to the audience can lead to some scary moments for Jonathan and other dedicated young dancers.

RENEE

Although he knows his job is to please the audience, Jonathan dances to please himself. He says he is an introverted dancer. "There are times when the audience downright frightens me."

Jonathan adds, "I want the audience to enjoy *Speeds*. I want them to laugh because we are laughing. If they do that, then we will become more comfortable. We're supposed to be relaxed and ourselves. I still might tighten up."

1:30: Carl is giving swimming lessons. Renee does leg lifts by the side of the pool. Gary demonstrates the back dive. Children swimming in the pool join in the fun too.

3:15: The bus takes the dancers to the theater. Debora finds a quiet place in the auditorium to warm up. Dancers begin to gather onstage. By three-forty Marilyn and Jonathan are practicing "Fast Duets" with Christopher.

Renee takes one look at the stage and gulps. The hardest thing for her will be to say "Change" loud enough for everyone in the audience to hear.

Jennifer begins the final rehearsal by making a few last-minute announcements. She eases some of the stress of opening night when she tells the company that she is not worried. She sees that the ballet is in good shape and ready to open.

Because the stage is very large, the choreographer concentrates on the spacing and the lineups. Once again they work on the opening walk, snaking the stage. Jennifer watches closely. "All right, let's look at the first line."

The dancers repeat the sequence. When they have finished, she says, "You were all spectacular in the beginning, but let's do it one more time, for luck."

Ange calls "Change" and sings "Wha-Pas" as the group moves around the large stage.

Jonathan misses a cue and yells, "Yeeewow!"

103

Marilyn protectively puts her arms around him and tells the group, "He almost made it."

Christopher commiserates with Jonathan. "It is a long run." Jonathan wants to try it again anyway.

Jennifer says, "Let's do it from your second jump, Marilyn. This is your first jump, Jon." They run their sequence one more time as the rest of the dancers watch patiently from the side.

"On to jumps," shouts Jennifer, galloping through the ballet. "AND . . . it's a yebababbab yump . . . yump . . . great." She sprints to another side of the stage. "Let's do the lift." Everyone moves quickly.

Jennifer saves time at the end of rehearsal to teach carefully choreographed bows. Then she says, "It will be up to Gary to decide whether to do an encore. He will either walk off the stage or—if he wants an encore—he'll signal you all by turning." She explains which parts of the ballet are danced in the encore.

The final rehearsal ends. Jennifer stands before her colleagues for the last time. It is a moment of pride and affection for these dancers who have worked so hard. She says, "Thank you all very much. Remember to have fun. I know it is going to be wonderful. I also know that you will be even better after you've performed it more. I'm not at all worried about tonight. We're not aiming for perfection. We're aiming for a first performance."

The entire group breaks into loud applause for Jennifer. She, in turn, applauds back. Keith says, "Ladies and gentlemen, we have a meeting downstairs in ten minutes."

Jonathan is still apprehensive. He worries that he doesn't know the ballet well enough. He worries that he isn't as confident as he must be to perform. He worries that he worries. "I continue to be obsessed until I've danced a piece on the stage twenty or thirty times. Then my body knows what the dance is. I think that is because I am still new to professional dancing."

Chaya, who has been dancing professionally much longer than Jonathan, is just the opposite. He worries *after* he is used to the ballet. "Our winter season opens in New York in December. After about six months, around May, is the most dangerous time for me. For the December season my memory is very fresh. In March I start getting tired. During April I try to hold on. By May my body looks for the easiest way to do the most difficult step. If I go onstage thinking that way, it is very dangerous. If I become bored, the audience sees 'boring' onstage. When that happens, I become frightened. I think, Who should I run to?"

6:00: The company meets to discuss travel arrangements. Tomorrow is the beginning of the Australia and China tour.

Final rehearsal

6:30: Chaya conducts the company class in an open area behind the stage. Starting at the *barre,* he leads a traditional ballet class. The mood is formal, serene. Birds are chirping; trees wave gently, reflected in the portable mirror that is set up for the class. As the company dances, Chaya walks around correcting form and position.

Chaya says, "When I was little, my mother took me to the ballet all the time. I didn't like it. I ran around the aisle. But I remembered those swans and *Coppelia.* In a few years I could sit through the three acts. I began to recognize beautiful lines.

"In the classical ballet classroom a dancer works on his line. Once onstage, it is still that *exact* line. The most difficult challenge for a classical ballet dancer is to do that line cleanly.

"Modern dancers study the same classic line in the classroom, but when we go onstage, we do the steps in a different way. We slightly, or maybe not so slightly, change them."

COMPANY CLASS

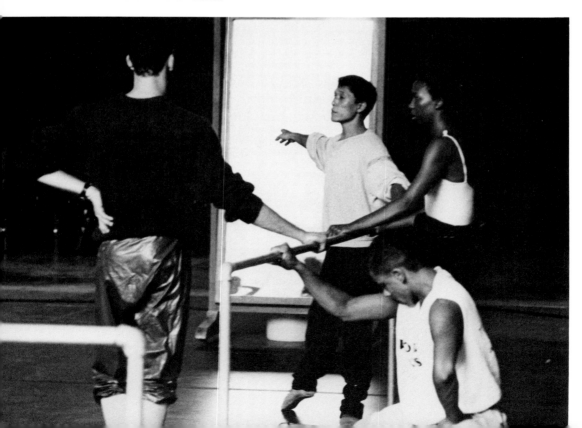

Marilyn

Neisha says, "It was hard in the beginning, and it keeps getting harder all the time. The more I can do, the more they expect from me—the more I expect of myself."

Marilyn and Jonathan remain onstage and run through "Fast Duets" four more times. Once they finish, Marilyn returns to her dressing room to shower and begin making up. Jonathan takes the second half of class. Over the loudspeaker Keith says, "LADIES AND GENTLEMEN, THE CALL IS IN ONE-HALF HOUR."

"That makes me nervous," says Marilyn. "I haven't yet found my makeup colors for *Speeds*. I'm going to wear the colors I use in *Stack Up*. Purple and pink. Pink makes me feel sweet."

There is a knock on the door. "Valuables?" asks a stagehand. Marilyn hands over some jewelry and her wallet. They go into a big pouch. She keeps working on her eyes by skillfully applying mascara to a double set of long fake lashes. "I learned to make up by experimenting. If I can make my eyes appear big to me, then the audience will be able to see them too."

107

"LADIES AND GENTLEMEN, FIFTEEN MINUTES, PLEASE. FIFTEEN MINUTES."

Marilyn shivers and continues. "This is the fun part, doing my face and doing my hair. Having my own dressing room is nice. I love it. I like to be by myself."

"LADIES AND GENTLEMEN, THE CALL IS TEN MINUTES. TEN MINUTES, PLEASE. THANK YOU."

"Ten minutes," she whispers as she puffs her hair. "I'm a very nervous person. When things get tense, I become nervous. I need to have my mind straight for everything that I have to do."

In the lounge outside the dressing rooms, the canteen is opened for the dancers and staff. People are sitting around drinking juice and eating junk food. Most of the dancers are in their dressing rooms. Jonathan is on the floor warming up once more. Ruthlyn sits on top of him, eating an apple. Chaya walks by.

"Thank you, Chaya-san, thank you," Jonathan sings.

Chaya winks as he walks toward his dressing room. "Keep warm," he tells them. In a matter of minutes Chaya returns wearing a long, elegant, black terry cloth robe. A thick yellow towel around his neck keeps him warm.

Jennifer, Christopher, and Ange return from the hotel showered, dressed, and looking ready for a first performance. Jennifer and Christopher place the champagne gifts on a long table in front of the company bulletin board. Ange gives the promised cast lists to Chaya and Gary.

"LADIES AND GENTLEMEN, THE CALL IS FIVE MINUTES, FIVE MINUTES. THANK YOU."

Jennifer, Ange, and Christopher leave to watch the show.

While *Lament* is being performed onstage, Debby stands in front of a mirror in the lounge and goes through all her *Speeds* movements. "Oh boy," she says as she shakes out her fingers. She sits down and sticks flesh-colored tape to the bottom of each foot.

Alvin Ailey walks by and asks, "Are you all right, Debby?"

"I'm fine. The bottoms of my feet are sore." The audience will never see the tape or have any inkling that she is in pain.

"I am looking forward to this," Debby says. "I think the audience will like it. It is our favorite piece. Even the dancers who aren't in *Speeds* are excited that it is part of our repertory. The atmosphere Jennifer created in rehearsals helped. It will be fun dancing."

Debby goes off to her dressing room. Elizabeth enters in full makeup but wearing her warm-up clothes. Off in a corner, she goes through her solo. "I am very excited. I'm sure everyone else is too. Knowing that Jennifer is there watching adds to the enjoyment. We all want to show her that it was worth all the work she put into it. I hope that she's pleased afterward."

The dressing room area becomes remarkably quiet. *Lament* music comes through the loudspeaker. Only Toni, the wardrobe director, works in the once bustling room. She wraps, organizes, and packs. Toni says, "Tonight is load-out night. My assistant and I pack each costume as the ballet ends. Costumes are organized according to ballet. By the last piece tonight, *Revelations*, the only things we will have left to pack will be the finale costumes. We are very organized. We have to be. It can get crazy. Absolutely crazy."

Elizabeth returns, looks in a mirror, and then leaves. She paces the hall.

Lament ends to a burst of applause. Next comes *Speeds.*

8. PERFORMANCE

9:25: Marilyn walks onto the edge of the stage to warm up. "It is peaceful here," she says. Jennifer oversees the laying of a shiny white floor. The stagehands work quickly.

9:27: Dancers begin moving onto the stage. Ange stands just outside the first wing, by the left side of the stage. A part of her is anxious about the oncoming event. Another part is bursting with pride. She thinks, I wish I were dancing.

Bill Hammond walks once around the stage talking to the dancers. He is nervous. "I am always terrified that everything is going to go wrong: The curtain is not going to go up; somebody is going to break a leg; the scenery is going to fall down; nobody is going to come."

Christopher moves about hugging dancers, inviting them to "have fun tonight."

Ralph puts his arms around Ange and says, "I want to thank you for everything." Ralph says he won't be nervous. He doesn't need to be; everyone else is. He observes, "The choreographers, the staff, the board of directors, everyone is very tense. I have to be calm and roll with the punches. When I see that loose energy flying around, I duck. I also pray a lot." Ralph is not nervous until the third time a new piece is done. "The first time is magic."

9:28: "Onstage, PLEASE," Keith calls. Ange is practically frozen in anticipation. Jennifer puts her arms around Ange. They leave with Christopher to take their seats in the orchestra. Bill gives one last check to see that everything is running smoothly.

"Maybe it's because we've been touring fifteen years, and we've seen everything go wrong at one point or another. Did we publish the wrong program? Did we print the wrong tickets?"

On a darkened stage the dancers begin to form into a circle. "Wait, wait, where's Renee?" someone calls softly.

"Renee, we need you," says Jonathan.

"Here I am." She hurries out to them while placing a hat on her head. Traditionally, before beginning a new ballet, the dancers form a circle and hold hands. They let the energy flow around the circle, bringing them together.

After a moment Danny says, "Bless us, Lord." Then the dancers go to their opening places.

RENEE

Debora says, "When everything comes together—the costumes, the lights, being on a stage rather than in the studio—there is an indescribable feeling. And then you remember there are people out there.

"My goal is to do the best I can. I always thank the Lord for what he's given me. Then I say, 'Please, don't let me fall.'"

WHOOOOOSH . . .
The curtain rises.

Chaya begins the opening walk slowly, quietly, the way it was rehearsed so many times. The dancers snake around the stage following Chaya as he moves faster and faster. A bright white beam of light covers him. They scoot off, Chaplinlike, leaving the stage empty. The theater fills with laughter.

A brilliant wash of color rushes across the stage. Chaya says, "To me, dancing is just there. That day. That moment. Then it disappears. Nobody can reproduce what I danced yesterday. Not even I. Wolf Trap seats three thousand people. The contact is direct, immediate. Then it goes. Only the wonder remains."

Each dancer runs toward the audience to say "Change." Renee tucks her thumbs into her lapels and lets out a resounding "CHA-A-A-NGE." Oh no, she thinks, startled. They are going to kill me for being so loud.

Danny whispers, "What was that?" Renee rolls her eyes and keeps on dancing.

In the audience Jennifer, Christopher, and Ange squeeze each other with excitement. Renee's "Change" broke through her stage persona to reveal her own dazzling personality. That is what *Speeds* is about—changing. Now they know the ballet will work. They noticeably unwind.

Renee and Danny begin "Slow Duet." Danny says, "I like knowing that I'm making an audience happy. That's the joy of it. I hope the people see something that uplifts and inspires them. If I've done that, I feel good."

112

IN THE WINGS

In "Fast Duets" Jonathan and Marilyn are bookends. Their jumps
are exactly together, their lines are straight and clean. The
audience responds. All those extra rehearsals were worth it.

Marilyn says, "Sometimes I ask myself, What am I doing here?
How did I become a dancer? It happened for a reason. And I think
it happened for a good reason. I want the audience to experience
our love and energy. That's why we're here. It is hard, but if you
want to dance badly enough, you go for it. This is what I want,
bad, so I'm going for it. And times like this I think, I'm going for
it pretty good."

Ruthlyn is sitting in the wings with members of the company,
some of whom have never seen *Speeds*. She is emotionally
onstage with her colleagues. "For me the stage is the ultimate
high. When I am onstage, I don't care about anything else. There
is nothing else. I transcend to other vast and wonderful places."

113

CHAYA/"CIRCLE DANCE"

CHAYA, RALPH, AND JONATHAN/"CIRCLE DANCE"

Danny and Renee/"Slow Duet"

ELIZABETH/SOLO

JONATHAN AND MARILYN/"FAST DUETS"

DEBBY'S SOLO/"MULTIPLES"

Gary's solo, Debora and Jonathan in click line/"Multiples"

"Coda/Folk Dance"

The ballet flies by—over, it seems, before it has begun. The audience cheers as the dancers take their bows. Other dancers, technicians, and crew in the wings are clapping and shouting, "GREAT" . . . "GREAT" . . . "LOVE IT." Backstage people are hugging and kissing one another.

Jennifer, Ange, and Christopher rush backstage. When Jennifer enters, everyone shouts, "BRAVO!" . . . "BRAVO!" The choreographer and her two assistants are beaming.

Alvin Ailey, smiling broadly, says, "Wonderful! Wonderful! Well done."

Bill Hammond comes running down with Keith, thumbs up. "You've got a hit here—wonderful!"

Jennifer, trying hard to avoid all the fuss, says, "Why isn't everyone picking up their champagne? Marilyn? Jonathan? Ralph? Where's Ralph?

"Ruthlyn? One is for you."

Ruthlyn says, "But I didn't *do* anything."

Jennifer tells her emphatically, "You will."

Renee comes in, still worried about her exuberant "Change," and asks, "Are you going to kill me?"

Jennifer says, "Kill you! That's exactly what I wanted you to do."

Renee throws her arms around Jennifer. "Thank you, thank you for everything you've done."

Chaya says, "This place has a lot of dreams. They are possible dreams. Many dreams are never going to become real. But in here, a dream is reachable. That's what makes the young people come to school every day. That's what fills our theaters. That's why I'm a dancer."

Over the loudspeaker, Keith calls, "FIVE MINUTES, LADIES AND GENTLEMEN. FIVE MINUTES, PLEASE."

The dancers disappear to their dressing rooms to prepare for the final ballet.

CURTAIN CALL

RUTHLYN

GLOSSARY

arabesque   The ballet position in which the dancer stands on one leg while extending the other leg straight back. The position of the arms can vary.

attitude   The ballet position in which the dancer stands on one leg, extending the other leg behind, in front, or to the side with the knee bent at a ninety-degree angle. The arms can vary.

barre   A railing, or "bar," that the dancer uses for support during exercises. *Barre* also refers to the actual warm-up exercises that make up the basics in ballet.

diagonal   Executing a step while traveling in a diagonal direction.

downstage   The area of the stage closest to the audience. The forward part of the stage.

duet   A dance for two performers.

extension   The ballet position in which the dancer raises and holds a leg in the air with the foot above shoulder level.

glissade   A gliding along the floor. The leading foot moves along the floor to depict a gliding motion. The second foot closes to the first foot.

humanistic   A dance approach that accentuates emotional and psychological relationships. Dancers interact onstage in a ballet that usually depicts a situation, a story, or the human condition.

line   The perfect body shape for a given position, which is the goal of every dancer. An idealized form based on classical principles.

penchée   The leaning or inclining of an *arabesque.* The body is forward while the foot of the raised leg is lifted to the highest point.

persona   From the Latin, *dramatis personae.* The stage presence adopted by a performer.

plié   A bending of the knee or knees from a standing position with control at the top of the leg so that the knee is properly placed in the direction of the foot.

pointe   Used in ballet, the action of being on the tips of the toes while wearing toe shoes.

post-modern   An avant-garde approach to dance that advocates pure movement or steps with no emotion, no dramatic overlay.

relevé   The action of pulling the heels up off the floor.

rhythm   A pattern of measured movement that consists of regular and irregular pulses or beats.

rond de jambe   The ballet movement in which the dancer moves one leg in a circular path, either in the air or on the floor.

score   A written presentation of music.

second position   Feet and legs turned equally apart and to the sides of the body forming a single line. The arms can be in second position also.

solo   A dance for a single performer.

tempo   The rate of speed of a musical piece or passage. The time. The beat.

trio A dance for three performers.

walk Technically called marking. A dancer "walks" through a ballet by rehearsing all movements and spacings, and conserving energy by not doing the lifts, jumps, and other fatiguing steps full out.

TECHNICAL INFORMATION

All the photographs were shot in natural light or stage lighting. I used a Leica M-4 and M-2 with a 35mm Summicron F2 lens, a 50mm Summicron F2 lens, and a 21mm Super Anulon F3.4 lens, and a Canon F-1 camera with a 100mm F2.8 lens. I developed and printed all the photographs using Kodak chemicals and Ilfobrom paper.